THE BABY
AND THE BATHWATER

Nina Coltart

THE BABY
AND THE BATHWATER

Nina Coltart

Foreword by
Christopher Bollas

INTERNATIONAL UNIVERSITIES PRESS, INC.
Madison   Connecticut

Acknowledgements

Chapter five, "A Philosopher and His Mind," is included in *The Mind Object*, edited by Edward G. Corrigan and Pearl-Ellen Gordon (London: Karnac Books; Northvale, NJ: Jason Aronson, 1995).

Chapter seven, "And Now for Something Completely Different . . .", is included in *Psychodynamic Supervision: Perspectives on the Supervisor and the Supervisee*, edited by Martin Rock (Northvale, NJ: Jason Aronson, in press).

Chapter nine, "Endings," is included in *Psychoanalysis at the Political Border: Essays in Honour of Rafael Moses*, edited by Leo Rangell and Rena Moses-Hrushovski (Madison, CT: International Universities Press, 1996).

First published in 1996 by
H. Karnac (Books) Ltd.
58 Gloucester Road
London SW7 4QY

INTERNATIONAL UNIVERSITIES PRESS and International Universities Press, Inc. (& design) ® are registered trademarks of International Universities Press, Inc.

Library of Congress Cataloging-in-Publication Data

Coltart, Nina.
   The baby and the bathwater / Nina Coltart ; foreword by
Christopher Bollas.
      p.   cm.
   Includes bibliographical references and index.
   ISBN 0-8236-0535-3
   1. Psychoanalysis—Miscellanea.   I. Title.
RC506.C616   1996
616.89'17—dc20   96-28318
                                                                         CIP

Manufactured in the United States of America

For Isabel,
with love and thanks

CONTENTS

ABOUT THE AUTHOR

Read Modern Languages at Oxford before training in medicine at St. Bartholomew's Hospital, and subsequently as a psychoanalyst while working in the National Health Service as a psychiatrist. Set up in private practice in 1961, and has had a mixed psychoanalysis/psychotherapy practice ever since; also rather specialized in consultations for diagnosis and assessment, leading to referral, and, over a period of thirty years, did total of just over 3,000. Has travelled extensively, including for teaching purposes in Australia, Sweden, and the United States. Retired at Christmas 1994. In retirement, does a lot of reading and writing, gardening, and, for part-time voluntary work, has become a Room Warden at Woburn Abbey, the local Stately Home. Has also been made a Governor of a local primary school.

Has written *Slouching towards Bethlehem: And Further Psychoanalytic Explorations* (1992) and *How to Survive as a Psychotherapist* (1993).

PREFACE

This is a collection of papers written (with one exception) during the last four years. In character, I suppose it is similar to my first book, *Slouching towards Bethlehem* (1992). That is to say, I would be hard put to it to describe a definite theme or pattern to the book, yet at the same time I recognize that it has a distinct flavour of "the sort of thing I write". The lack of an underlying theme is probably because I write most often in response to requests from various people or organizations, who may say that they would like a particular sort of paper, or to hear more about something I have touched on previously; *or* the request arrives at a time when I have been thinking about a certain subject, and I am quite pleased to go on doing so. I very rarely write a paper with no external incentive.

It will be evident why the first paper is in that position. It *was* my first paper, written in 1967. It does demonstrate that I have always greatly enjoyed constructing a paper on a clinical subject. It seemed natural then to ask "Why Am I Here?" and, having explored that, to give a brief titular description of how I experience the clinical situation, namely "Two's Company, Three's a Crowd". Then there is a simple teaching paper on technique, "Handling the Transference", which leads naturally in to my favourite sort of writing—that is, clinical case histories: "A Philosopher and His Mind" and "Blood, Shit and Tears", which also contains a longer theoretical section than I usually provide. Then an introduction to a change in clinical scene, "And Now for Something Completely Different . . .", which is a paper about two contrasting sorts of supervision, but which also leads on to a change in subject matter, "Buddhism and Psychoanalysis Revisited". This returns to a theme in my first book. "Endings" is where it is largely by reason of its title, although it is an intrinsically clinical paper. Strictly speaking, its title might suggest it as the closing paper, but since this is, in all probability, my last book, I wanted the last chapter to be one in which I look back over thirty years of psychoanalysis and reflect on what I left behind during those years and what I brought on with me, or initiated later; hence its title—"The Baby" being what I retained or what has grown along with me, and "the Bathwater" what I threw away. This paper and "The Man with Two Mothers" neatly bracket the others, as themselves being the first and the last of my writing life.

FOREWORD

Christopher Bollas

T his book follows a very special calling. If, as Nina Coltart says, she writes in response to "external incentive", those who invite her to give a talk serve as useful mediators of a strangely far-off and yet intimate other to whom she speaks with respectful ease and who, she knows, takes her for who she is. If it is, as she says, "in all probability, my last book", we should protest if she follows the literal meaning of her sense while at the same time acknowledging that this book is written against the other who gives birth, hears from us through life, and then takes us in our death. To hear this invitation and to write a final group of essays is to meet a particular literary challenge.

These essays are luminous autumnal visions of her life as a psychoanalyst as she reflects on its beginnings—here at Bart's Hospital—its middle period at the British Psycho-Analytical Society—and now, in retirement, in the reflective hollows of her country garden or in the musing shadows of Woburn Abbey. She calls herself an "armchair traveller", and this book is a unique entry in the genre of travel literature which is closest to the English heart. Often she takes us back to a recent past that she, perhaps rightly, thinks we will have forgotten—though surely not the Triumph automobile, which, she feels, she must explain! But a "Decennial"? Know what that is? "A Decennial is a meeting attended by people who all qualified, or joined a firm, or started doing something momentous for them, at the same time", she tells us. It is a reunion, and her description of her talk—"A View from the Couch"—at the Bart's Decennial reflects the "cheerful, ready-to-laugh atmosphere" of the event, but also, like photos of a departed generation of people gathered at a festive occasion, it is a moment of wonder and affection: the transient festivities of a life are poignant punctuation marks of what a strange journey this all is. "Ever since early childhood", she tells us, "I could think of nothing that gave me more intense enjoyment than listening to people telling me their stories", and this is evident in these travelogues, which contain vivid stories of her work with patients. "Imagine to yourselves the confusion that all this represented to the mind of a young analyst in the early years of private practice", as she embarks on the story of her treatment of a patient with ulcerative colitis. He "had not been a welcome baby", she reckons, and her account of his anguished offensiveness is both moving and amusing at the same time. An episode from the tale:

> I would say he was showing signs of dreading the coming holiday and the separation from me. "Nonsense!" he would roar, "what a bloody-fool idea. You're so *conceited*, that's one of the things I can't *stand* about you—oh, I must go to the loo." And he would bound off the couch. Some minutes later, he would return, looking pale, sweaty, shaken, but unmistakably triumphant. "There you are!" he'd say fiercely. "I'm bleeding again, see what you did. I haven't bled for three weeks, why can't you keep your fucking ideas to yourself?"

"You will begin to see here", she writes, "something of how his language was so crudely concrete and graphic that it, in itself, spoke volumes." And she adds, "and also you may begin to believe that I look back on this patient as the *noisiest* patient I have ever treated". If this scene from her travels shows us the vexed labour of two people who are stuck with each other in a Harold Pinter world, the "you" to whom she tells this story is not simply those of us who hear this story, but beyond us—perhaps within us—that other to whom she speaks with frank relief. "One day I said something simple and, to me, obvious about shit and his penis. 'Don't *use* those words', he screamed, wriggling furiously; 'I can't *stand* that sort of language, I think you're *disgusting*'." She doesn't have to tell us what she thinks about it. Like all great travel literature, it is conveyed in limpid observation.

Her accounts of patients are, however, never at their expense. If she finds pathos in their suffering, it is because in these people—who have indeed lived very different lives from her—she discovers a puzzling and challenging oddness that makes not only what she has to offer, but what psychoanalysis can provide, problematic. Is this why, out of hundreds of patients she has selected for this book of endings, she chose some of those people whom she could only partly reach? Her colitis patient's aunt (mother's sister) and first cousin died of colitis. When he was 11, his mother developed a carcinoma of the breast. Coltart the guide tells us, "This would have been in 1946. She had a mastectomy and the rather crude radiotherapy that was all there then was available." His mother's symptoms recurred when he was 13, and with metastases in the liver and bone she lived upstairs for another eighteen months. The site of the operation and the other breast became involved in fungating secondaries. "Many readers will not have seen this; today it is very rare; but it was, indeed, a disgusting sight and it smelt."

Her comprehension not only of this patient's mother's illness but his own colitis—and her understanding of the organic ailments afflicting some of the other patients in this volume—is a most persuasive case for our need for medical psychoanalysts. Nina Coltart does not plead this cause, but her grasp of the body's own logic, and of the encounter between the afflicted and the affliction, is informed by medical knowledge: knowing how the vulnerabilities of a body foreshorten existence is part of her unsentimental compassion for the pathos of this patient. "Recently, I tried very hard to find him, for the sake of this paper, but he has even, significantly, disappeared from the Medical Directory, and I think that one must conclude, in view of the severity of his illness, that in all probability he is dead." Probable, yes. But an epitaph written with lucid, controlled prose that ends one of the most compelling cases to find its way into the psychoanalytic literature.

Coltart writes about the life of another doctor, this time one who was hopeless as a psychoanalytic training candidate and thankfully returned to general practice after qualification. "She would present an excruciating, detailed session of confused dialogue that was not like anything I had ever heard before, not even like conversation, which would have had its own mild value", she writes. "Bits of undigested theory, odd technical words, startling and confused ideas, which she had hoovered up at random during the last few years, were strung together in a muddled stream"—certainly unlike Mary and Anne, an inexperienced counsellor and an experienced psychotherapist who came to her for supervision and with whom it was a pleasure to collaborate. Her description of how she "set out with them on a new journey of discovery" as they learned more about psychoanalysis from her is a great read.

And then there is "Elizabeth Cameron", the senior training analyst who decides to do a one-year group training at the Institute of Group Analysis. Coltart's observations on her middle self—which never makes a true debut in the group but is the unceasing object of the chapter—is a witty and wily account of why a psychoanalyst is after a while no longer able to be a good group member. Her deft private observations of the other members of the group are as amusing as her account of her falling to pieces and needing group support over uncommented-upon empty chairs is moving.

Her illuminating chapter on her voyage into Buddhism is refreshing and "full of acute psychological observations", as she says of the Buddha. Indeed, it brings to mind a certain feature of Coltart's own sensibility: a still concentration and then a distilled verbal rendering of experience. Whether she is writing about her experience in a group, with a hopeless supervisee, a brilliant but fated philosopher–suicide-to-be, or life in the British Society, her compositions are still-lives. Like Vermeer—one of her favourite painters—she reflects the people and places she has seen, but in her own unique light.

Juxtaposed to the light surrounding her characters is what she terms the "clarifying light" of intuitive perception. "There is a strong sense" in such a moment "that one's conscious mind is not the prime mover in what one sees, or knows, or says." "It is as if one *is lived* from depths within oneself for a brief period", she concludes, to which the reader of this book may add a further observation: that when we read a work of this depth—one that does not blithely dismiss the surface manifestations of life's characters, but finds appearance inspiring—we are lived by the depths of *this* prose.

Nina Coltart was one of the great training analysts, supervisors, teachers, and administrators at the Institute of Psycho-Analysis from the early 1970s through the mid-1990s. An outspoken critic of dogma, her forthright defence of true independence of mind earned her widespread regard for her courage and integrity, and she was rewarded in the best possible way: a steady stream of self-referred patients found their way to her doorstep. No analyst—no five analysts combined—ever saw as many people for consultation during her career as did she, and her care to ensure that those who consulted her were "well placed" meant that she followed them up, hearing how their consultation had gone, and eventually being informed how the analysis had gone when ending some years later. Thus she came to know an extraordinary number of psychoanalysts and psychotherapists and, of course, came to know who were the truly outstanding clinicians, those who were good journeymen, and those who were not good enough to practice. She managed what was, after all, a considerable powerhouse of knowledge admirably well. One might hear on the grapevine that she had confronted a clinician who had done *poor* work, or, alternatively, find from a colleague that she was very pleased to see how the patient's analysis had turned out, but I think the community of analysts and therapists who relied upon her for referral—and upon whom she relied—valued her service to the community (of patients and therapists) in southern England. It is a customarily unheralded service, but such people do become legends in their own time—I think of Semrad in Boston—and when she left London in 1994 for her country home—and the next step in her journey—Nina Coltart left behind a country that was the better for her.

And if this is her final book, she has left the best for last. Psychoanalysts trained within the Independent Group are often asked by psychoanalysts and psychotherapists abroad which book they should read to get a feel for the way Independent psychoanalysts think and work. In the past one has referred to Winnicott's *Playing and Reality* (1971), Rycroft's *Imagination and*

Reality (1968), Khan's *The Privacy of the Self* (1974), and Marion Milner's opus—her several autobiographical studies and *The Hands of the Living God* (1959) are an unparalleled accomplishment and, as a literary movement, are the best expression of that independent thought "typical" of this psychoanalytic sensibility. But if we are to have *one* book, *this* is it. We may say: "Here, you will find it here." This work is a literary spirit of place—a beautifully rendered conjuring of sensibility—and to my mind it is the single best expression of the English psychoanalyst of independent persuasion we are ever likely to have.

THE BABY
AND THE BATHWATER

CHAPTER ONE

The man with two mothers

I am including this paper because I think it may be of interest at this point, when my writing life is coming to an end. It is the first paper I ever wrote in my analytic life, and after it I did not write another for fourteen years. I hope I am right in judging it worthy of inclusion; it is a sort of curiosity, though it shows much of what I recognize as familiar in my interests, and in my writing style. I have retained my use of the present tense in describing the course of the analysis as, to my mind, since the analysis was still proceeding when I wrote the paper, this is appropriate to it as a living process.

One of the ways of being assessed for full membership of the British Psycho-Analytical Society used to be to read a paper to the Membership Panel, which consisted of about twenty senior analysts. I read this paper in 1967, having qualified in 1964. [My next paper was "Slouching towards Bethlehem", in 1981.] My life-long enjoyment in writing about clinical material is already present. Some of the theory, and its language, now seems old-fashioned, compared with how I would think and write today. My recent classical training is much in evidence; but it has coherence and seems adequate to its task.

In publishing the paper, I am also expressing gratitude to the referrer and to the patient, both of whom are now dead. The referrer was Dr Denis Martin, the Superintendent of Claybury Hospital, who thus entrusted me with a considerable therapeutic challenge; the patient was a disturbed, psychologically minded, and thoroughly decent man, who taught me more than any other single patient has. It was he who led me to say to generations of students that if they could possibly treat a perverse patient early in their careers, they would never regret it, whatever the outcome, as they would have learned so much.

Introduction and history

Mr A was introduced to me in October 1963 by the Medical Superintendent of a mental hospital, who had seen him as an out-patient at the request of a general practitioner, with a view to admission. The Superintendent thought that although he presented a psychiatric emergency, he could be helped by immediate psychotherapy. After the crisis was over, Mr A decided that he wished to continue in full analysis, which therefore started in November 1963. He was 36 when he came to me, an unmarried schoolmaster, and at that time he denied any previous psychiatric history.

I should like to try to show how the effects of his intricate intra-familial relationships and certain events of his early childhood are demonstrated in the development of his sexual and fantasy life, and how this, in turn, has manifested itself in his analysis.

He was the only child of two middle-class Welsh school-teachers: his father married his mother only because she was pregnant by him, and they then separated. The mother went to live with her two sisters, one of whom was the matron of a big mental hospital. Mr A was born there and was breastfed and cared for by his mother for one month. As far as he knows, he was not a problem feeder during this time. He was then fostered to a childless working-class couple in London, who had a relative who had been a nurse in the above-mentioned mental hospital.

For the rest of his first year of life, he was an extremely difficult baby, failing to thrive, vomiting back nearly all his food, and constantly crying: indeed, we have come to know from some of his more regressed patches in analysis that he was in truth a "mad baby", and we use this concept of Winnicott's as our shorthand for his experiences then, and in these periods in analysis. He could barely assimilate what was good in his foster-mother until he began to establish some sense of separateness between himself and her; his primary world was so devastated by the power of his hungry rage that the imminence of total destruction only receded when he could begin to be aware that an indestructible "not-him" source of supply existed, and when he gained some measure of control over his body and its orifices.

Shortly after his second birthday he went into hospital to have his tonsils out. Also at that time he had an infection of the penis, due to phimosis (having an excessively tight foreskin), and he retains a memory of having his foreskin manipulated by a woman doctor wearing rubber gloves, who cleaned his penis with very hot water, while his foster-mother held him. He was aware of a conscious belief from this time on that his penis was bad and deserving of this sort of treatment, a belief reinforced by his foster-mother's attitude to his subsequent enuresis and preoccupied masturbation. He went to hospital again at the age of 8, with scarlet fever, and was not allowed to be visited, as was then the practice in isolation hospitals, as they were called. The memory of this time is like a confused but detailed nightmare of heat, desolation, injections, and enemas. He had a woman doctor again there, and he became convinced that both she and the nurses took pleasure in doing various uncomfortable things to his body. Since he could not understand why his foster-parents never came to see him, he evolved the theory that his illness and this segregated treatment was a punishment for being bad in some way; we already know that this badness was centred on his penis; an already-existing confused fantasy about the badness and undesirability of his whole bodily contents (namely what he had done to his internal objects) was now reinforced by the apparent desire of the doctors and nurses to get rid of these contents by enemas. Nevertheless, by a combination of projected ambivalence and reality sense, he conceived of the idea that although the female staff were enjoying punishing him in these ways, they were also genuinely doing it for his good and trying to make him "better"—an ambivalent word in his vocabulary. As one might imagine, there has been a considerable amount of analytic work devoted to his thoughts and feelings about my own motivations in treating him, indeed in being an analyst at all, which are not without value to my own self-assessment. The psychosomatic imprints and their fantasy elaborations which derive from these memories are all incorporated in his later perversion.

From his second to his fourteenth year, Mr A spent the month of August with his real mother in her home town on the South Coast, when his real father would sometimes also come to stay. His real father seems to have been a lively and debonair man, who meant well by his son up to a point, but had no conception really of how to put his vague good intentions into action. Mr A admired him and has either inherited, or identified with, his somewhat wry sense of humour, which has in fact, as an ego feature, stood him in good stead. He was less frightened of his real mother when his father was there, but at the same time remembers a pall of guilty unease, which overshadowed an occasion when his father took him out for the day alone, away from his real mother. This, it seems, was a direct homosexual anxiety, combined with a fear of the mother who wanted each of them, but totally and separately, for herself.

He has an odd and vivid memory, from the age of about 4, of his mother and the mental nurse sister poking in a dog's ear and making it yelp with pain. He is sure his mother really enjoyed this, and to escape from his anguish and the pain of his identification with both her and the dog, he went out and got lost on the pier. Although he enjoyed the relative affluence, the spirited conversation, the books, and the glamour of his real mother, he became on these holidays increasingly aware of an underlying dread that he would not be allowed to go back up to London to his home, and to his poor, but safe and loved, foster-parents. Until the age of 7, when he was enlightened by a school-teacher, he consciously believed that he had two sets of parents, and felt superior to his contemporaries on this account, albeit strangely singular.

In his tenth year, he broke down into psychosis. The immediate precipitating factor was a series of doctor–and–patient games with little girls, in which he examined them with a hungry intensity and growing fear and excitement at the sight of their genitals, and at his wish to get right inside them. His somewhat precarious hold on reality was undermined, and he became convinced that he was entirely bad, that he had *done* something irredeemably wicked, that the inanimate world was invested with hostile life, and that he was being mocked and derided by everyone, in danger of punishment from an all-seeing God, and quite alone, without hope of rescue. He refused to go to school for two terms and remained at home, not communicating any of this to anyone because he knew that if he did, he would be either killed or locked in a madhouse. He knew quite a lot about madhouses from his real mother's sister. I think the school refusal was not only because of his fear and sense of persecution, but also because "knowing" anything became taboo. It is clear that although an unconscious sadistic fantasy was already operating, he was also motivated in these games by an intense curiosity, partly stemming from an unsatisfied curiosity of childhood and partly from what Sants (1964) has called his early "genealogical bewilderment". What he came to "know" in these games was not only that mysterious castrated beings really existed, but that he was punished by both foster-parents and teachers for his activity. There have been times in the analysis when he becomes what I can only call stupid and "unable to know", and we have gradually come to see that at these times he is withdrawing either from some image of me as frightening, or from some approach to a sadistic greedy fantasy. He recovered from this psychosis due to such ego strength as he already had, combined with a non-comprehending but loving support from his foster-parents. He then returned to school and led a relatively normal life, to outward appearances, until the summer of 1963, when he was 36.

He did not maintain a relationship with his real parents after adolescence: his father died when he was 18, and his mother in the third year of analysis, when he was 39. His foster-mother died when he was 26, and his foster-father when he was 35. His deepest grief and mourning was for his foster-father, and this was, and still is in some degree, accompanied by guilt at having put him into a geriatric ward for the last two years of his life. I believe it to have been this mourning period that made him vulnerable to his breakdown in the following year; he became especially receptive then to the idea of life after death, or other incarnations.

At the age of 26 (after his foster-mother had died), he developed an active perversion with the girl who had nursed her, and he has maintained it ever since. It is a complex ritual in which he is strapped onto a table and held there, he imagines, by a shadowy woman; he is naked and imagines himself to be in a torture-chamber, which in turn is in a madhouse, surrounded by instruments of torture. He visualizes all this with hallucinatory clearness. The girl masturbates him fiercely, pricking his penis and scrotum with needles and burning them with matches; she wears a white coat and rubber gloves; she mocks him verbally at the same time, saying humiliating things, but in a tender, loving voice; and she also reassures him that this is all for his own good; she ridicules his "penetrating" her, which he does with his right hand, while the left is strapped down to prevent him from tearing at her breasts; nevertheless, he tells her that he *is* doing this, and oscillates rapidly between shouting obscenities at her, to confessing abjectly his total badness and guilt, and pleading with her to castrate him. When he ejaculates, he feels badness go out of him and goodness flow through him, and he is "restored to himself". This used to take place about once in three weeks, and he had no other relationship with this girl. Her remarkable plasticity in having adapted to his demands so absolutely and for so long has, of course, reinforced his belief in his omnipotence, since to all intents and purposes she is his creation.[1]

He has a steady non-sexual relationship with another girl, which has run parallel to the perversion for many years. With her he lives a close life, as in a companionate marriage, but they do not share a house.

---

[1] As I have learned more about psychopathology in the last thirty years, I have realized that it is by no means uncommon for a patient with a perversion that requires a partner for its enactment actually to find one and to establish a relationship with her, which depends solely on the perversion for its continuation. It is not a friendship, and they do not meet for any other purpose than to enact the perversion. It is clearly mutually gratifying, and the two have an extraordinary, almost wordless, capacity to recognize each other almost at first glance.

A third girl-friend, who was my type physically, existed in parallel with the first three years of his analysis, and she in some ways served implacably as a very direct transference resistance. She would give him dinner, and they would occasionally masturbate each other without fantastic elaborations. Although it was only slowly that he came to see how he was splitting off and acting out with her some of his more "straightforward" infantile longings, I consider that his use of her in this way may also have facilitated his bringing of other difficult material into the analysis. Words and descriptions have so often felt to him like literal and concrete objects that a certain dissociation from too intimate a contact with me was probably of value to him. None of these three girls knew about any of the others, such was his capacity for conscious compartmentalizing.

Alongside his perverse activity with the first girl, Mr A's. sexual activity is, until recently, confined to masturbation. He has always felt the need and compulsion to masturbate before sleep, such as another person might feel about saying his prayers: indeed, for Mr A the two activities have much in common. He was very religious until the breakdown that preceded his analysis, and his God was a harsh, watchful judge. Mr A's conception of God was moulded by his going with his foster-mother to a primitive evangelical chapel as a child, which seems in his recollection to have been filled with women, apart from himself and the preacher, whom he anyway muddled with God. These women would wail and moan, and often sing about being washed in the blood of the lamb. The whole scene became intensely exciting to Mr A, redolent as it was of the strangeness of women, their lamenting, which seemed to have something to do with *being* women, and their conspiratorial, if bloodstained, relationship with God, which he felt was denied to him and yet was also, in some inscrutable way, his *fault* for having damaged them. His nightly masturbation, aimed at "getting the badness out" before sleep, was intermingled with prayers for absolution and has always been more ego-dystonic than the acted-out perversion; I take this to be partly because of having to contain his sadistic superego—in spite of attempts to place it "out there" in God—and partly because of real memories of having been punished for masturbating, which literal condemnation the perversion ritual escaped. This repetitive, guilt-laden masturbation, in which he constantly gains both sexual pleasure and punishment for it, exemplifies, I think, Freud's point in "The Economic Problem of Masochism" (1924c), when he says that the superego "is as much a representative of the id as of the external world".

In the summer of 1963, Mr A went on a course run by the Scientologists, who used semi-hypnotic techniques to induce a state of vulnerable suggestibility and florid fantasy, and who then "explained" the fantasy contents by allocating them to previous incarnations of the individual concerned.[2] Mr A had an intensely felt hallucinatory experience with a woman "auditor" in which he was attacking and murdering a naked woman, branding her breasts and splitting open her belly; he simultaneously felt his own body attacked. He was plunged into a state of terror, guilt, and confusion. One may infer that the Scientologists, having apparently no knowledge of dynamic psychology, do not allow for the fact that one might bring one's superego with one from a previous incarnation. Mr A started with me two days later, with the statement that he felt as if he was utterly mad and fighting for survival.

The analysis, and theoretical considerations

Mr A is a well-built, good-looking man, with expressive features and a tendency to blush. He is an excellent raconteur, which, together with his highly developed sense of humour, have as-sisted in producing a successful sociability: at times he beguiles me into laughing at one of his stories, and invariably we then find a wealth of meaning in the joke, reaching to the most primitive levels of his fantasy life. His analysis has been characterized throughout by a strong co-operative drive, which, since it is always somewhere present, facilitated the handling of some of his most violently negative and resistant periods, also by a certain resilient fortitude in weathering turbulent and painful patches of

---

[2] This was in the days before Scientology had been discovered by journalists and come to public attention. It serves, nevertheless, to give us some idea of why, when that did happen, the press they received was a bad one.

experience, and in working through them with a grim tenacity that is one of his most valuable ego traits. The difficulty in internalizing and assimilating good objects means that there is a considerable amount of three-steps-forward-and-two-steps-back in his working-through processes: this, of course, in its turn is related to the oral nature of much of his pathology and to the effect of his own oral aggression turning on, and attacking, anything good that he has allowed himself to ingest.

It is clear that Mr A has been preserved from psychosis by his perversion, in the manner suggested by Glover (1933): "Certain perversions are the negative of certain psychotic formations and help to patch over the flaws in the development of reality sense." But his protection has not been complete. He has known about the strangeness of his inner world for years, and often had a conscious dread of breakdown. He has had periods of depersonalization. He has been afraid of ever getting angry. He has been aware of the necessity for restriction on his activities, and he has felt shame and frustration at his inability to have a normal sexual and family life, though the perversion itself is not consciously a source of shame. Indeed, he has always regarded it, perhaps more rightly than he knows, as the most important thing in his life. Gillespie (1956) points out that the ego-splitting involved can salvage a sufficiently important part of the ego for the services of reality adjustment. Nevertheless, I visualize Mr A's. ego not only as split, but even in the adequately functioning area as having some rotten floorboards, and under severe stress he is at risk of falling through them into a terrifying underworld of violence and part-objects. The whole theory of pre-genital development, of component instincts, and of part-objects has been illuminated for me by the content of this underworld of his and has made the study of Freud's *Three Essays* (1905d) a vital experience.[3]

---

[3] I can remember precisely the learning experience I am describing here. I wonder what it would have been like, and how I would have phrased it, if Mr A had started treatment with me in 1993 and I had qualified in 1994. Probably no better; there is an elegance and simplicity about the theory that I was using then which makes it attractive, and I am not convinced it has been improved upon by subsequent ramifications.

Mr A almost immediately formed a very strong transference relationship, which has continued with unabated intensity, often in the psychotic mode. I was, at the outset, his good rescuing foster-mother, but this speedily brought to the fore his deep and constant childhood anxieties, which we subsume under the heading "Betrayal". If he chooses one mother, he is guilty of having betrayed the other, and each in his inner world can react accordingly: his foster-mother with grief and hurt, his real mother with contemptuous rage. Thus early was the stage set for the development of a certain sort of paranoia, when one of his split introjects would be felt externally as persecuting and enraged, and also as invested with his own deep sense of having been betrayed by his primary mother.

It became clear early on that it is largely his idea of his real mother that provides the fantasy-object of his libidinal and aggressive pre-genital impulses. Freud's paper on Leonardo da Vinci (1910c), with its study of the two-mother-effect, helped to illuminate here the deep ego- and object-split in Mr A in relation to his mothers; as did also Winnicott's (1954) concept of the object-mother and the environment–mother, though he is referring to them combined in one person. My earliest view of the transference phenomena was that, broadly speaking, Mr A's. fantasy elaboration of his real mother was the object-mother, and his foster-mother was the environment mother: nevertheless, there also turned out to be an intricate network of instinctual drives relating to his foster-mother. Inevitably, at times in the transference I would alternate from one to the other, and he soon began to suffer the guilty pain of "choosing" one, by reason of the implied sadistic attack by him on the deprived, unchosen other. This particular circumstance soon provided a facilitation of the linking of many extra-analytic phenomena and relations with the analysis and myself. I should like to describe here some of the ways in which the details of the history, as narrated in condensed form in the first section, began to be unravelled through the medium of the transference; and then go on to a broader consideration of how we have developed and understood them within the analytic framework.

About three weeks after the beginning of the treatment, Mr A had a dream, in which I came to him with my mouth open for a kiss, and he thought in the dream "she really isn't afraid of anything". This meant nothing to me at the time, and so I did not interpret it;[4] but since he had made veiled references to his violent feelings, and how he felt, paradoxically, that they were frightening to him, but also "cleaned out" in his perversion (which at this point I knew very little about), I formed the idea that the perversion was serving as an isolation defence method, and also one in which perhaps he could achieve the undoing of something destructive or "bad" that he felt he had done. With this in mind, I persisted in trying to interpret blocked silences and somewhat shallow remarks as his attempts to resist bringing into the analysis something that he or I might be afraid of. A fortnight later, he was complaining that I seemed to be "standing about inside him, watching and being forbidding". He said I had become the "eye in the triangle", which is a Masonic symbol of God. He belongs to the Freemasons, and I should like to refer to this again later. I commented on the ambiguity of the eye/I; and I asked what it was that I was having to help him defend against. He cried, and with great shame and difficulty told how once he and his girl-partner had bought a hamster for a specific purpose, and this purpose was that she had held it, and he had pithed it with a needle though its open mouth. I then related this to his dream, and to his fear of becoming so sexually excited and enraged with me, whom he was "buying for a specific purpose", that he might destroy me. This produced considerable relief of the defensive anxiety, and we were able to link it meaningfully with the real mother's forceps going into the dog's ear, and the tonsillectomy instruments, and later the enemas, being forced into him. He has never done anything to an animal since that one occasion.

The relief of this tension, however, ushered in a long phase when, although he was able to bring more freely material containing affect and depth, I was alternately felt as a Godlike superego and an attacked hamster/person. I was still considering the idea that he had to use his perversion to "clean" himself, which suggested something more anal than had presented itself so far: Mr A in fact began to talk at that time about the burning sensation of the defaecation that followed the enemas, and on one occasion I tried a possible link between this and the burning and

---

[4] The wisdom of ignorance!

branding of the breasts in the fantasy; the next day, he inexplicably and suddenly became upset because he did not like the fact that I had freckles all over my face and arms. Now, as a matter of fact, although I was tanned from a holiday, I do not have freckles, and I said so. I asked who had. His real mother was very dark and always had heaps of freckles, he said. I said tentatively, not wanting to push the interpretation to too primitive a level too quickly, that perhaps when I was an attacked mother, my breasts were branded with pieces of burning shit. As I was to discover in the course of time, he was often there before me with this sort of interpretation, and he said at once with real comprehension, "You know, I always really did think her freckles were bits of shit."

During this phase, which covered about the first eighteen months, he abandoned his belief in God, which was a relief to him, though, I suppose inevitably he sometimes looked back to it regretfully and felt that it had been a good thing; sometimes it was something that I had stolen from him; however, the biggest experience was of liberation. I had not been exactly aware of being embattled with God, until he told me that I had won. I was somewhat apprehensive that the failure of his God would mean that I would be felt as *more* harsh and watchful, but this did not happen; instead, there seemed to be some increase in insight and in reality sense, and a reduction in anxiety about coming to sessions. When we were thinking about the chapel he used to go to, he said one day that although he still had to contend with *my* blood, at least I wasn't now covered in the blood of the lamb, which I said I thought meant a hope that neither he (Mr A) nor anyone else would have to be sacrificed to me. He made another connection here, when he added, "Lambs are branded when they go to the slaughter." It was through this that he first began to be aware of the deep fusion by projection and identification that existed between us, since in his ritual it is he who goes to the slaughter, but I, the breast/woman, who am branded.

Between eighteen months and two years after the beginning of treatment, he began to talk a lot about his current school, which hitherto had not featured very much. It became clear that he is a gifted teacher, and his special interest is in bringing on difficult and backward boys of 10 and 11, which clearly he now wanted me to know, and which I interpreted as his way of dealing with, and repairing, his damaged self at that age.[5] This made sense but produced little other response, until I began to see that the admiration that he gets from the children at school was gratifying to an inordinate exhibitionism, while I, who at that time—still unconsciously to him—was felt to be ridiculing him, was neatly preserving a *status quo* by, in conjunction with the gratification there, deriding him and thus giving him the expiatory pleasure of punishment for his exhibitionism. A part of his fantasy was thus being enacted through these parallel experiences, in that he was receiving dual gratification. The scorn was consciously being directed by him at me, and I was quailing somewhat under it, until one day he linked his vision of me "sitting complacently here at home doing nothing" with his self-image of showing himself to be wise, and, what is more, powerful, at school. I suggested that by being so contemptuous of me and my meagre offerings, he was reversing a process that he was afraid of masochistically enjoying, in which I would be felt to be humiliating him for his small, yet really dangerous, exhibited erection.

This was accepted after a while, and a period of comparative calm and ego-work ensued, until I became a liar. This was just before and after Christmas 1965, when he had been in analysis for twenty-seven months. Because of his separation anxieties, I had hitherto given him my address during breaks, which he had appreciated and not made use of. At the approach of the Christmas break, 1965, I made what I now think was a wrong decision not to do so; I made a note at the time to the effect that I did not think he needed it so much, though I have had more thoughts about this since. In any event, it became apparent, not so much that I was being forgetful or depriving (which were bad enough) but that I was lying to him, and that retrospectively my previous

---

[5] On the educational front, we hear quite a lot today about children with special needs, special trainings for Special Needs teachers, etc. Mr A was completely unqualified; he had been neither to university nor to teacher-training college. "Special Needs" had not come into being. Fortunately, for several years after the War, people were taken on in schools to be teachers simply as a result of applying for jobs, such was the shortage of personnel available. Thus, someone as obviously gifted as he was enabled to follow his vocation creatively, without wasting years being told how to by less gifted tutors.

gestures of "wanting to include him in" had not been "true". All my words and attitudes became suspect, and, not helped by the fact that I genuinely felt I had made a bad mistake, I blundered about in this morass for some weeks. Interpretations of the early traumatic separation and change were of no avail, nor of me felt as a sadistic depriver. Eventually I grasped the idea that although he had consciously enjoyed his holidays with his real mother (up to a point), he was now more aware that there had been a constant undercurrent of "something wrong" in the atmosphere, that he had been lied to, covertly and by implication, by her; he was given the impression that she enjoyed him, and indeed his maternal aunt often told him that his mother wanted him back, and that he should "choose to come". The Lie was that he knew that at an early age she had given him away, and did *not* want him. It was in working out the implications of this episode of the Lie that we came to unravel two threads of the perversion. One, the lesser one, was the meaning of the mocking contemptuous words spoken in a tender loving voice—that is, one or other of the attitudes herein expressed must be a Lie. The other and more significant thread was the uncovering of one of the layers of meaning of the whole ritual, namely its ultimate defence against castration-anxiety. Throughout the ritual, he experiences great castration-fear—indeed, throws himself on the side of the fierce castrating mother by begging her to do so (and thus get it over); but always in the end there is the point at which it is just avoided: the Great Threat was a Lie. Our mutual understanding of this situation finally enabled the analytic process to change gear again. For a while he felt, luxuriously, that he might be able to hate his real mother, which he realized might allow for the possibility of loving instead of carrying out a reciprocal Lie-act: this had a considerable direct effect in that it reduced the need to act out his sadism extra-analytically.

The paramount clear-cut manifestation of the anxiety surrounding choice and betrayal was in relation to holidays. First came a guilty dread at leaving me, as his foster-mother, for his "summer month" with his real mother. But this soon deepened into the area where I was at the same time his excitingly cruel mother abandoning *him*. A characteristic pre-holiday session after eighteen months' analysis opened with his saying how he felt a deep dread that he would not see me again, and that his

belly was aching and felt hollow. (He used to somatize extensively, and still does at times.) I said: "I've not gone yet, but you
have already attacked me so much that I feel only like a bad,
hurtful thing to have inside you." He began to get angry and said,
"I was just feeling so good last week, and as if you were a real
good person I could rely on. Now you're not even bad, don't flatter
yourself—you've *gone*, don't you see?" I showed him during the
course of this session how it was his own magical power allied to
his fury that devastated his world of anything good.[6] He then
embarked on the next stage of this procedure, which was to start
battering me with what he calls "simple, straightforward questions", demanding an immediate answer. On this occasion, the
question was, "Am I mad, or am I not?" and his fury mounted as I
continued to try to analyse the need for this sort of questioning at
such times. It was clear that, since he knew I didn't "answer"
such questions, he could in this way create a vehicle situation for
his wrath at me for being neglectful, depriving, and abandoning
and both re-enact, and avenge himself for, some of the misery of
his first year of life. Nevertheless, this interpretation did not by
any means penetrate to the depth of his emotional turmoil: it was
finally when he spat out: "If you'd just tell me *something*, so that
I'd know", that I arrived at an understanding that in a world of
crying and helplessness, the beginnings of knowledge—that is,
conscious knowing-about-himself and the world—must have felt
like life-saving food that he could have, and keep, and assimilate
into himself. This was typical of many times when we worked over
this ground of his rage arising from hunger and *my* betrayal of
him; the more he raged, the badder I became, until he reached a
point of total destructive rejection of me and was then starving to
death, since, although a bad breast/mother, I was also unique
and the only hope of survival.

   As a result of later libidinal and fantasy development, together
with his real experience as outlined earlier, this sense of badness
of himself and all his internal objects have become especially

---

   [6] This phraseology is an example of how close I still was to the
influence of the training. There is a certain sort of analytic presentation
that is very fond of saying: "I showed the patient such-and-such. . . ."
Very soon after I qualified it began to seem to me to be an all-knowing, *de
haut en bas* way of speaking, and I have never used it since.

focused on his penis, which he is then totally identified with—
that is, he loses a sense of whole-self, and himself becomes a
part-object. He used to "clean himself" of this mad rage by going
away and acting out his perversion, thus protecting me, as a
remembered but temporarily lost good object, from destruction:
after about a year of analysis, elements of the perverse ritual
began to appear much more markedly within the analytic session. He would feel me not so much as actively leaving him, but
as actively punishing him then and there; he would hear my voice
as powerfully deriding, and on several occasions he hallucinated
the smell of urine, faeces, and menstrual blood in the room,
which I was smearing on him. I am felt to use these as weapons
not only because he himself does so, but because his secret plan
is to tear my guts out with his penis, and there is thus a rough
justice in my using their contents to punish him.

It was through some analytic working-over of this transference appearance of the perversion that the reparative wish,
concealed behind the sado-masochism of the ritual, was gradually revealed. It was only if his guilt at his rage and greed could
be expiated by me, as the castrating punisher, that he could be
restored to me. I, as the excitingly sadistic but castrated mother,
am felt to be taking back the penis which he not only attacks me
with, but has torn off me in the first place: he can only repair me,
and this persecuting, bleeding wound, by giving up his penis—
and therefore, by identification, himself—to me again. Since there
is, of course, a deep and total confusion in him of the breast with
the penis, the restoration of his penis/self to me means also the
healing restoration of my breast to him. Thus the reparative wish
itself was combined with a self-preservative drive. Towards the
end of a session in which we had done some intensive work on
these lines, he said: "I dreamed last night that I was angry with
you because you weren't treating me properly, we weren't getting
on; but you said we were, and to prove it you showed me your
mouth and hands were wet. I couldn't see your teeth, but I don't
think you had any. In the dream, I felt you needed me in some
way to care for you." His associations were: having always
thought of medical treatment as being with hot water, and he
recalled the penis manipulation; his childhood enuresis, to which
he added, "I suppose you've been washing my pants ever since I
got here"; his terror of the vagina as having a sort of portcullis in

it, which would clang down on, or behind, him; and a sudden revival of a lost memory of a post-office money-box he had had as a child, which had a teeth-like arrangement in the slot so that you could get your money in but not out, and which he had smashed open with his foster-father's hammer and then felt too guilty to spend the money, for fear that the God-like Post Office authorities would get him.[7] He thought it might have been milk on my mouth and hands. I took this dream in its full context to be concerned and constructive, filled with a longing for a reunion with a good breast/mother undamaged by his biting penetrating sadism—or, rather, able to be repaired by him instead of retaliating with all the violence of his projected sadism, which would thus gratify his harsh superego (which also contains this breast/mother). A paper on homosexuality by Pasche (1964) describes the theory in which the mother treats her son like a penis that she does not herself possess. She wants to make herself complete while dispensing with her husband: he is the organ of replacement of a being which repairs itself at his expense; as soon as he detaches himself from her, he perceives her as a very frightening castrate. Hence his anxiety. Mr A in his fantasy exemplifies this absolutely, though he has elaborated it, for in spite of his phallic imagery the strongest libidinal and aggressive elements are oral.

It was through the detailed analysis of the complexities of the perversion fantasy, as it thus appeared in the transference, that we came nearer to recognizing the nature of his very secret vision of an ideal state. He now calls it the Circle, and it incorporates a third, idealized mother. This has evolved in relation to myself at times when he experiences me as combining qualities that were good in both his mothers, cemented together with a magical idealism and uncontaminated by his fear, rage, and greed. The Circle consists of himself at my breast and with my arms around him, and his penis in my vagina. This state of blissful fusion is again predominantly oral, since he is feeding me with his good penis, in accordance not only with early unconscious fantasy and breast/penis confusion, but with his actual belief for some years during adolescence that his semen was milk. Khan's paper on

---

[7] This now strikes me as one of the most brilliant bits of free association, and retrieval of a lost memory, that I ever heard in thirty years of full-time practice.

"Ego Ideal, Excitement and the Threat of Annihilation" (1963) has clarified my understanding of this deeply hidden area in Mr A and of the way in which the perversion itself acts as a defensive structure against loss or breakdown of the ultimate and longed-for Circle. It is both strong and vulnerable, since I, his creation, am maintained as the breast-for-him by his being the breast/penis-for-me.

During his fourth year of analysis, and following upon such work as already described, and also on the death of his real mother, we began further to unravel his distorted Oedipus complex; that is to say, there was a reduction in the defensiveness provided by the perversion against the implications of the Oedipal situation (Gillespie, 1956), and it became more accessible. One of its major distortions is that Mr A has had to contend not only with an Oedipal father, but with the persecutions of whichever mother he abandons in choosing a heterosexual object. The father in the three-person relationship internally is a compound figure, comprising elements of his real, admired father; his foster-father; his foster-grandfather, who is remembered chiefly for having an enormous penis and for having once thrown a bucket of water over two copulating dogs; together with many accretions from his own oral, anal, and phallic sadism. Mr A has come to see how powerfully and magically he felt he had separated his real parents himself. For a long time his homosexual and competitive relationships with his father were held away from me through the medium of the Freemasons, to which he belongs. It was seeing me one day in a car with a man driving that jolted his Oedipal anxieties more precipitately into his own awareness of the transference. Hitherto we had been deeply involved in the earlier pre-genital relationships, either of narcissistic fusion, or of two persons, or part-persons; if he experienced me at all as being other than his personal object or part-object or self, it was as a lesbian; though this, too, filled him with a corrosive envy of the loving and mysterious breast-relationship I had with another woman. He came to see that it did, however, protect him from Oedipal jealousy. Shortly after seeing me at this time in the car, he took to arriving ten minutes early and thus encountering on different occasions two male patients, one rather baby-faced and one whom he called Bluebeard; at first this nickname was consciously just because this man had a beard, and he did not at once associate to the fairy-tale Bluebeard's sadistic sexual promiscuity. He did not comment for some days, and then he suddenly attacked me for giving them extra time and keeping him waiting. He was astonished when I pointed out his wish to watch us and intrude on us by coming early. He then said: "I feel I ought to hate that baby-face more, but I really feel *murderous* towards Bluebeard." I said that, of course, *he* was the one I had intercourse with, rather than fed, and, as occasionally happens with great suddenness in a session, he fell away from his reality sense and into his psychotic transference state, in which my statements became literal,[8] and his own words concrete objects. He stiffened his body and ground out through clenched teeth: "I could *kill* you." Mr A is on occasion capable of arousing real alarm in me, and this was one of them. I interpreted that I was to him at that moment the terrifying woman of his fantasy, taunting him with the badness and smallness of his penis. He said, "You wait, you wait till I get mine into you, I'll split you open and kill you." I said, "But you're trying to do it right now, ramming your words into me, and terrified that you're going to succeed." With this, he surfaced again, as he normally does if I manage to reach the fear behind the rage; but this brief exchange, of extraordinary intensity, illustrates how steeply he drops away from the threatening Oedipal situation in the transference to the wild fantasy world where only he and I exist, and in which language ceases to be inferential and symbolic and either disappears or is experienced as weapon-like excreta.

It was striking how further unravelling of the refracted and bent component instincts in the context of the Oedipal situation (Sachs, 1923, quoted by Gillespie, 1956) led both to improvement in his outside life and to a deeper regression in the analysis. He has recently, after years of rather paranoid battling with his Headmaster, come to like and admire him and has been promoted to head of his own department. He also allowed himself to be put up for election as Master of his Masonic Lodge, and he was elected. As may be imagined, the secrecy of the Masonic ritual from women has served as one of his major resistances in the analysis, but as time has gone on he has come to understand

---

[8] I had rather invited this reaction, I suppose, with the over-economical directness of a "literal-sounding" interpretation.

much of the psychodynamic meaning of this secrecy, and the defensive need to split off this "secret area" from me has been much reduced. I therefore feel justified in regarding advancement within the Masonic brotherhood as part of his improvement and integration, since it represents an amelioration in his relationship with both male authority figures and male peers.

He has also managed to sell his foster-parental home, in which he had lived on since their deaths, fixated there by his dread and guilt at destroying them forever, internally, if he abandoned them. It was this last action particularly that contributed to a profound re-experiencing in his analysis of some of his earliest states of being, the memory of which has lived on in an imprinting in his body-ego. I refer especially to a state of being that is, I think, what Winnicott means by a "freezing of the failure situation", which Mr A has endeavoured to "unfreeze" in the analytic environment, and which he has both consciously and unconsciously hoped will make adequate adaptation to present need, where, in the far past, he could not.[9] The hope itself, which is for survival, at the time of the re-experiencing was not conscious, since the essential state is one of remote despair, but it can be inferred obliquely from the capacity to re-enact the time when it, the hope, was felt to be absent—namely, part of his first year of life. It seems that at these times, when he becomes literally very cold and speechless, he requires me to be, not so much an "auxiliary ego", as *his* ego, and through my supplying such functions as perception, conceptualization, description, and interpretation he is able to "have" areas of himself that are deeply pre-verbal and to integrate them by re-internalization of my/his ego in its special capacity as a secondary processor. In this way, I think he is both using a meaning of the Circle, and also growing beyond his need to maintain it as his secret and unattainable goal.

As he grows beyond it, he is faced anew with the problems attendant upon independence and separateness from his objects

---

[9] I must confess that I am not entirely sure what I was saying here. I remember Mr A's occasional lapses into coldness and inability to think, but perhaps my attempt to explain the sequence of events is rather too condensed.

and with an increasingly painful awareness of how stunted is his capacity for love, concern, and gratitude. This latter was elegantly illustrated this summer [1967]. He had been quite severely disturbed at the approach of the long break, and I arranged to see him twice in the middle of my holiday. This filled him with pleasure and hope and what appeared to be gratitude; but when the time came, he failed to appear. Recent work this term (the Autumn term) has shown that the failure to appear was a piece of acting-out that remained entirely unconscious: he was deeply shocked when he got a letter from me commenting on his absence and trusting that all was fundamentally well with him; he had, indeed, "clean forgotten". It transpired that, having had the *promise* of the sessions, he was gratified (not grateful), triumphant, and satiated. The sessions themselves had been irrelevant. He had a marvellous holiday, never felt better, and in this state, in which genuine improvement mingled with borderline mania, he had had "normal intercourse", but with his perversion partner, for the first time, on one of the days when we had planned a session. This at least points to some of the huge aggression in the act of forgetting. We are only now beginning to unravel the extensive ramifications of this episode.

Prognosis

Mr A's consciously expressed hope, and belief, is that he will eventually be freed from the extensive and complex ties of his past, as represented succinctly in his perversion, to enter upon a normal sexual life in which he will marry and have a family. I confess to sharing the hope rather than the belief, though further experience may teach me otherwise. He is aware that in many modes of his being he now has far more enjoyment and freedom from psychic pain and anxiety. The changes in his experience of himself and his world are solid enough to justify this hope: my difficulty in sharing his belief is related to a quantitative assessment of the trials of his formative years, and of the many derivatives of his pre-genital fixations, which are still manifesting within the transference. Needless to say, his analysis continues.

Postscript, 1995

Mr A ended his analysis after eight years. I am glad that I had shared his hope but also that I was more sceptical about his chances of ever having a "normal" sexual and family life. He gave up the acting-out of his perversion, and his need for frequent masturbation diminished. He tried to develop a sexual relationship with his "companionate marriage" woman, but this, of course, was a failure. In the end he came to understand, and accept, "limited gains".

Where Mr A continued to advance was on the ego-front. He achieved a long-held ambition in obtaining a degree—in psychology—from the Open University, and with this behind him he embarked on a training in a new field, closely allied to our own, and then worked in it successfully; thus the gift to which he had earlier given expression with difficult boys was enabled to come to full fruition in a most satisfying way.

He kept in touch with me with a letter every Christmas, in which he described a reasonably happy life, with many friends and a sense of fulfilment in his work. Nevertheless, who can judge what lasting damage he had suffered, psychically and psychosomatically, and under what degree of stress he still lived? He was well and active to the end, but he died suddenly of a massive coronary while still only in his early 50s.

CHAPTER TWO

Why am I here?

S ometimes I wonder. I am not asking one of those huge
ontological questions, like "Is there a Purpose for me in
the Overall Plan?" or "What is the Meaning of Life?" Many
people ask themselves—and other people—variants of these at
different stages of their development, and a few seem to find
answers that satisfy them, usually in the sphere of religion. My
question is localized and specific. I have spent the greater part of
my waking life, since I built up a full-time psychoanalytic and
therapy practice, sitting in an armchair either behind a patient
on a couch, or facing a patient in another, similar, chair. The idea
of the armchair traveller comes to mind; and travel we do, and
not only when a patient returns from a long journey, or when we
take our holidays. We enjoy the ever-new fascination of travelling
deep into inner space, both ours and the patients'. The people
with whom we go need a companion, and—sometimes without

This paper was first written for a Westminster Pastoral Foundation
presentation in 1993.

In order to avoid too much repetition, I try to refer, throughout this
paper, to "therapy" (occasionally "analytic therapy") and "therapists", to
indicate people who have been dynamically trained to practise as psychoanalysts or analytically orientated psychotherapists.

23

any clear idea that this is what they are doing—they ask us to go with them. Why do we offer to accompany them?

Oddly enough, I did not give much thought to this question at the beginning of my life as a therapist. I felt completely sure that it was what I wanted to do. I shall say more about this certainty later. The question can crop up in various ways, and one of the first I came across was about twenty years ago, when I was asked to give a paper at the Bart's Decennial Club evening. A Decennial is a meeting attended by people who all qualified, or joined a firm, or started doing something momentous for them, at the same time; they gather for a reunion. The events being celebrated cover entry from a block of ten years at a stretch—hence "Decennial". The Bart's Decennials are always enjoyable, convivial occasions; two or three people are asked ahead of time to prepare papers either on their specialities, or about a particular piece of work they have concentrated on during the last ten years. I went to the second Decennial that was available to me, by which time I had been an analytic therapist for about ten years. And at this point, by the definition of my own analyst, Mrs Eva Rosenfeld, I was just about ready to call myself a psychoanalyst. This definition first appeared on the day I qualified (as it is called), when, of course, I was still in my personal analysis. I was in a relaxed, rather triumphant mood, on the couch, and enjoying the sense of achievement—when my analyst said in her blunt way, taken from her own analyst, Sigmund Freud: "Right—now in ten years' time you will probably be a psychoanalyst." Incidentally, I am so far a unique product of the Royal Hospital of St Bartholomew, which tended to produce general surgeons and specialist physicians, especially paediatricians and haematologists, and recently oncologists, but—with only a couple of marked exceptions—not psychiatrists, and certainly never psychoanalysts. As far as I know, I am still the only psychoanalyst they have managed.

I called my presentation "A View from the Couch", and instead of what I feared could become a rather boring, and perhaps incomprehensible, essay on psychoanalysis and how I got there, and so on, I wrote very little text, in which I made some jokes and sounded a light-hearted note, and I illustrated it lavishly with slides. Each slide followed hard on the heels of the last, and each was of one of the numerous cartoons about psychiatry and psychoanalysis which are such rich subjects for cartoonists the world over, and which I had collected for many years. I would say something like: "Of course, one has to learn to assess a patient's psychological state, and often convey something of one's opinion to him—next slide, please—", and along came that familiar old chestnut: "No, you haven't got an inferiority complex, Mr Smith— you *are* inferior." I managed to describe quite complicated therapeutic manoeuvres and supply some detail about psycho-pathological states, as I had a huge collection of cartoons, many of them applicable to various different subjects, including thera-peutic techniques. Thus I included one, for example, that turned out to be about the biggest hit: a posh therapist in a grand room is sitting behind his couch and saying to the large, elegantly dressed man who is lying on it: "Now you're a little boy of three again, Sir Hereward—all except your bladder, that is." I used another of the cartoons as the cover for my second book, *How to Survive as a Psychotherapist.* An analyst is looking in a bewil-dered way, from his vantage point, at an empty couch. The patient is lying underneath the couch.

By the way, have you noticed that two universal staples of these cartoons are (a) a framed diploma or certificate on the wall, and (b) a note-pad and pencil in the therapist's hands?—both of them things that, at least in our branch of the profession, we would never have at any price. At least, I am taking it fairly confidently for granted that we wouldn't—and yet cartoonists seem to feel they are essential to recognition.

In the cheerful, ready-to-laugh atmosphere of the Decennial, "A View from the Couch" was a success, and this may well have emboldened me to start writing in earnest a year or so later; and writing—always about case material or points of technique— always has, since then, felt as if it has been an integral part of the complex structure, composed of so many different elements, that go to make up—or confirm, rather—Why I Am Here. Also, in a way I had not encountered before, questions came thick and fast from the floor following my paper at the Bart's meeting and included—I suppose inevitably, in that gathering of what I call "proper doctors"—"Why did you choose to do that?" and "What are you *there* for, really?" I imagine that I scrambled together some answers, but since that day I have often thought about what those questions evoked in me; one of the first things I realized was that, although accidental, it was right that those two particular questions came together. They are closely linked, although they do not refer to the same thing.

That is, "Why did I do it?" connects up with "What am I there for?" but I do not think it necessarily always does in quite such a unitary way. It depends on the personality, and inner attitudes, of the therapist, on the original meaning of the choice, the motivation, even the philosophical stance. It was perfectly possible that at the point of the Decennial Meeting, when I had about ten years' experience behind me, the complex motivations that had prompted me to set out on that journey might have radically changed, and in ten years have changed into motivations to *continue*, which were quite different. As it happened, this was not so in my case, but I knew some therapists for whom it was true then and for whom it is true now. They go on doing therapy because it is there, rather like climbing Everest; it is simply what they do, and after a few years they couldn't do anything else with any degree of skill. Although this attitude may be to some extent true of most of us, it is more like that of a businessman going to the office. I do not intend this as a criticism; a businesslike attitude to one's job, whatever it may be, can be productive of detailed efficiency. But who is to say whether it is better or worse than the retention of excitement and wonder, and some of the other more emotionally coloured states that I had felt in the beginning—and at times still do?

One person during that discussion asked if I had wanted to be different from everybody else at Bart's. I could not answer this except in a rather long-winded way. It certainly wasn't a primary or strong motive, but I did have a sneaking liking for being different from other people (don't we all, I ask myself now); however, in regard to this choice that we were talking about, I truly thought that difference from all the others was irrelevant. As an immediate urge to action, or a long-term feature, I cannot think it would be very sustaining. Another enquirer wanted to know if I had been attracted by the prospect of making a lot of money, indicating by his question that he was possessed by the widespread misconception, amounting almost to a myth, that therapists are fabulously rich. I had enough information right at the beginning not to subscribe to this myth, and the early lean years were proof, had I needed any, that I was far worse off than if I had continued up the promotional ladder in psychiatry, which I had abandoned in order to enter the field of therapy. I said that most of them were probably doing far better than I financially, and that as N.H.S. consultants, with a solid N.H.S. pension at the end of their working lives, would continue to do so forever. But such is the power of myth, I do not know whether I was believed.

After the Decennial, I continued to reflect on the two questions that had been raised, with the intention of clarifying my mind. One of my strongest and deepest reasons for wanting to be a therapist was that, ever since early childhood, I could think of nothing that gave me more intense enjoyment than listening to people telling me their stories. There is an important distinction to be emphasized here; I do not mean *any* stories. I never cared much for fables and fairy-tales and sagas. I still don't. There is a type of novel that has become rather popular and fashionable, under the general description of "Magical Realism". Examples are the works of Angela Carter, Salman Rushdie, and Gabriel Garcia Marquez. Fantastic elements play a part in them—animals talk, people fly—bizarre incidents of this nature. I find this aggravating, to say the least, and it gives me no pleasure to read. Life can be quite bizarre enough in its ordinary course. The story I enjoyed had to be from the teller's own life and experience. The dawning awareness that it was possible to do this for a living was quite slow in me. I am not sure that the superego did not have something to do with the slowness; could it be true that something that seemed to offer pure pleasure could also be called one's "*work*", in inverted commas—and actually enable one to be *paid* for it?

Fortunately, it did gradually become convincingly apparent that people not only like, but need, to tell their stories, especially to an attentive listener equipped with certain skills. Such skills assist in creating the next chapter when some painful, confused climax has become the sticking-point of the narrative thus far. Of course, there is a spectrum of cathexes involved; the natural raconteur, who is usually already fairly mature in object-relations development, will obtain some direct gratification from telling his story, even while maybe crying with the overall sadness and suffering in his account, whereas the person who is naturally reticent, who tends to silence rather than speech, is described as someone who "never talks about himself", and uses a different set of defences from the first type, will experience severe difficulty, will have to be helped and prompted, and will rarely obtain any immediate sense of relief at unburdening. Technically, the first type is probably a hysteric and the second schizoid. Hysteria, though it has become downgraded through misinformed popular use, is a useful and valid term for a quite advanced stage of development, whereas the schizoid character arises from an intensification of a certain developmental state that occurs earlier in life. But on the whole, whatever the characterological development, human narcissism is such that there is very rarely *no* benefit at all experienced through a concentrated presentation of the most absorbing of all subjects—oneself.

From time to time, one meets somebody who says the following, or a variation of it: "I wish I had your job. It must be pretty nice just to sit all day listening to people, not feeling obliged to do anything much about them or even speak to them at all unless you feel like it." Of course, in a slightly sinister way, this caricature of our working lives comes rather close to the truth, and to one of my strongest and deepest reasons for wanting to be a therapist—that is, liking listening to people's stories. I find that, as is usually the case, the soft answer turneth away wrath (the wrath, not uncommon in the speaker of such words, usually arises from a sort of malicious envy, itself based on ignorance and fantasy.) I tend to say: "Well, it's not quite like that . . ."—and, indeed, it is not. But one can hardly embark on a description of the subtle richness that informs the art of listening, and of how many interlocking psychic manoeuvres it contains. I have written of these elsewhere (*How to Survive as a Psychotherapist*, 1993, chapter on Paradoxes), and, as that chapter-heading suggests, I have seen these psychic manoeuvres as inherently paradoxical. For example, one is focusing directly on what, and in what way, the patient is saying, yet at the same time scanning the whole situation, and the surrounding content and mood; one studies the nature of the transference as it manifests each day, and at the same time scrutinizes oneself for one's own reactions and signs of countertransference. One is intricately related to the patient and his inner-object world, yet one is also detached in order to be able to reflect on them, and on oneself both as subject and as the patient's object. It is these and various related paradoxical states that constitute the therapeutic skill in the act of listening and provide a continuous challenge and source of interest for the listener. There is another popular myth, which I have already touched on—that telling one's story, "getting it all off one's chest", is inherently healing; this is essentially the idea of catharsis, but I do not think it is always true. Apart from the people I have referred to who find it very difficult, and whose efforts may be followed not by relief, but by shame or a sense of loss, I do not believe that pouring it all out to a picture, or a dog, would have a cathartic effect at all. Therefore there must be something essential in the act of *telling another human being*—and, I would add, one who listens in a particular way, not just any old human being who may have none of the learned paradoxical skills and may anyway be preoccupied with affairs of his own. This is the argument against people who are scornful of psychotherapy and hold the opinion that "talking it over with a friend" is just as good. Apart from the facts that a friend has not developed the skills, that the context is rarely conducive to confidences of a certain sort, and that a very particular sort of trust has to be developed slowly in the special contexts we provide, there is the danger that if one embarks on this kind of thing, one will soon find one has not got many friends to talk it over with.

In connection with the remarks from people who envy the simplicity of our job, "just sitting all day listening to people", I am inserting this passage two years after writing the original paper. I have now been retired for six months, but I still see, on occasion, certain long-term patients whose lives would have been very much impoverished by a completely arbitrary termination of their relationship with me. These are often people who are in some fundamental ways so scarred by life that the loss of a person who had become of special importance to them could set them back a long way after the years of careful work we had achieved together. Why I refer to them here is that the sessions with them really bring to my attention that we use a lot of (presumably psychic) energy in our chosen therapeutic work—more than I ever would have thought to be the case when I was doing it all day and every day. I notice that I have to make a real effort to adopt the "third ear" listening stance and, even more, to think and speak in the reflective, interpretive, "analytic" way that used to be second nature to me. I enjoy these sessions, and would not now abandon these few people for the world, having made the decision to go on seeing them indefinitely; but they are tiring, in a way that nothing else that I now do is, in the peaceful atmosphere of retirement.

The specialized, highly skilled, and complex listening, which can take a long time to learn, is one of the primary reasons why I am here. It was a skill I wanted to learn, partly to promote enjoyment in listening to stories, and partly because it is something intangible, immeasurable, and invaluable to give to people who are in need, who very often make one feel peculiarly powerless. What this—healing—wish was about for me I will say in a moment. But first I want to add a little more to my description of the skill itself. As we listen to a patient, for the first or the 500th time, we observe with our inner, image-making eye that he is laying out pieces of his personal jigsaw-puzzle for us to ponder over; as the patient speaks, so we process the pieces, both consciously and unconsciously, recruiting theory and free-associative imagination to help us in the task. And for us, the task is continually absorbing, filled with challenge and revelation, repeatedly testing our mettle; I do not believe that I could ever be wearied or bored by a task such as this. And a job that does not hold the prospect of boredom sooner or later is rare, and to be highly prized.

Intuition, so relied on by Bion that he was prepared to back it as the vital element in all analytic therapy, leads us into and through the deeper inner worlds of the patient and comes into its own when silences fall between the working pair. Then, if it is one of those good days when one's own machinery seems to be in top working order, one may be ready to speak into that silence almost at once. Very occasionally, as intuition shines a beam of clarifying light straight onto the darker recesses of assembled puzzle pieces and all our strategies combine to form the next interpretation, there is a strong sense that one's conscious mind is not the prime mover in what one sees, or knows, or says. And, of course, it is not. It is as if one *is lived* from depths within oneself for a brief period, depths that one can trust, and which yield up the nearest thing to "inspiration" that we ever experience. The patient shares in its creation and, at such moments, is open to receive what emerges, resistances abandoned. A form of communication is in process which it is almost impossible to describe or define accurately. Perhaps it should be called meta-communication. These are peak experiences and cannot be summoned by the voluntary will; we can only continue faithfully to work to the best of our ability and prepare the ground for their occasional arrival. But when it happens, it is memorable, and worth working and waiting for; I cannot imagine any other work that could produce these unique moments as often as ours does.

Let us proceed to another, perhaps less obvious, answer to the question under review: Why am I here? Psychotherapy is about relationships. The early papers of Freud, when he was setting out so much that was—and is—important about analytic theory, convey a lot of information that was later to be defined and discussed in terms of object-relations theory, yet from Freud himself there is a distinct, and at times rather eerie, sense of paradox about them. For years, Freud wrote from the viewpoint of one-person psychology (that is, the patient's), in spite of having "discovered" transference, which is essentially about two-person psychology, as far back as his days with Breuer in the late nineteenth century. It is in his papers on technique (written between 1912 and 1914) that Freud began to demonstrate his instinctive—rather than theoretical—grasp of the importance of what later came to be more incisively defined as "object-relations theory". This was the work of analysts such as Klein, Fairbairn, Balint, and Winnicott. At present, the most vivid and readable writer on the whole subject is Christopher Bollas. And, recently, David Scharff, Director of the International Institute of Object Relations Therapy in Washington, D.C., concentrated on bringing British Independent Group analysts over to the States, and introducing object-relations theory and technique to the American literature. But, in spite of the distinct object-relations flavour of his technique papers, Freud mainly continued to concentrate on the unitary workings of the patient's psychological structure; for example, although it was he who introduced ideas about projection, these did not progress, then, into an expanded awareness of interacting inner worlds constructed of internal objects, nor did he have very much to say about the dynamic connecting implications of the therapist's person and presence. One-person psychology, in theory and in modes of thought and expression, continued to dominate our field for over thirty years, through the enormous influence of Freud, who was patriarchal, didactic, and intolerant of rivals. There is something quite amusing about the sustained adherence to one-person psychological theory, while writings about transference and the influence of early important figures in the patient's life, by the Freudian contemporaries, were also on the increase. I sometimes wonder how on earth I worked as a therapist without object-relations theory; it was really only in the 1960s and 1970s that it became widely available in journals and books, yet it has always been taken as a self-evident fact that prospective therapists are drawn towards their chosen field because their interest in personal relationships is of paramount importance to them.

By the way, this is not the same as saying that psychotherapists are good at "human relations", which is a more abstract, sociological subject. Indeed, they are not. It is another of the paradoxes of our professional world. It is often, I am sorry to say, sharply evident to lay people outside the profession—especially when members of our professional organizations are operating as representatives *of* the profession. As a group, our handling of relationships with the "real world", whether social, political, or on any other level, leaves a great deal to be desired. Frequently it is distinguished only by clumsiness, lack of worldly sophistication, patronizing authoritarianism, or paranoia. There is a marked insensitivity to the feelings of others, redolent possibly of an inadequately matured narcissism; all this comes as a disillusioning revelation to people who, at the very least, expect of us that we will be rather specially skilled in human encounters. I think our inadequacy in this respect may well be connected with something that Neville Symington was finally bold enough to say in his recent book (1993). He is of the opinion that a long personal analysis, which we all have as part of our training, leaves the narcissism stronger, and the ego weaker, than they were at the beginning of analysis. This is a condensed comment, and a significant one, and it repays a lot of careful thought. Only then can one decide whether one agrees with Symington or not. I certainly do.

Rather as one might expect, the atmosphere inside psychoanalytic societies only serves to increase one's understanding of their ineptness in handling the real world. There is a considerable amount of gossip, and a readiness to believe malicious hearsay about one's colleagues, accompanied, rather naturally, by poorly handled paranoia. Analysts, who are entrusted during their daily work with confidential material to a degree even exceeding that of the priest in the confessional, are not trustworthy or even ordinarily decent in their relations with each other. With a few notable exceptions, I would never expect an analyst to be loyal and supportive to me through thick and thin, if a subject at issue happened to be one that rouses such an analyst to unnatural pitches of defensive frenzy and his opinion did not concur with mine. This could be true even if he had appeared amiable and friendly in some social situations; the ordinary bonds of affection and trust that hold friends together unchangingly, even if they happen to disagree over some matters, do not seem to develop between analysts, meeting, as they do, either at conferences or seminars or, more likely, on the numerous committees that have burgeoned in our growing bureaucracy.

Some of the unpleasantness of the atmosphere is due to the uneasy cohabitation of groups whose theories differ deeply, many of whose adherents feel bound both to proclaim and defend them with a fanaticism bordering on the religious. Analysts like to think of themselves as scientific and detached, yet the members of different theoretical schools all too often bring apparently unworked-through passions to their views on psychic development. Lamentably often I have heard it said, of someone bold enough to criticize a passionately held theory, "Oh well, of course he/she isn't really properly trained", or "isn't doing real *analysis*". Is it any wonder that a young analyst, unsuspecting, who steps naively into one side of a controversy and encounters this sort of demolition from some heavyweight senior to himself, begins by feeling hurt and shocked and goes on to develop a sort of anxious paranoia?

The Controversial Discussions, as they have become known, were recently edited and published by Pearl King and Riccardo Steiner (1992). They give the detailed picture of the British Society in a state of open civil war, between the (Anna) Freudians and the Kleinians. It was probably both bold and correct to publish them, but they are by no means edifying, especially to anyone who has tended to idealize psychoanalysts or at least hope that they may be rather mature and thoughtful human beings. The war is supposed to be long over, and it is true that an uneasy, shallow peace has reigned for some of the time since those years. It is said that the tension nearly split the Society completely, and it is supposed to be a triumph for some sort of "British diplomacy" that we all stayed together, fragilely protected by a cumbersome, ultimately irrational device known as "the Gentleman's Agreement". Along with several others, I have often failed to detect any advantage gained from our still being one Society, in which an unpleasant undercurrent of internecine sniping still goes on, inadequately concealed by the ingratiating and untrustworthy personal interactions to which I have referred.

In spite of this, and however it comes about, we come to "be here" in the first instance through a combination of personal factors that include, almost always, a lifelong curiosity about other people, and a desire to know more about how they function, what makes their engines work, how one understands abnormalities and suffering that have no obvious cause—to name but a few. In some people, this combination of factors can authentically be called a vocation and is experienced as such. I believe it is valid to use the concept of vocation, about our choice of psychotherapy as our life's work; it is limiting that the concept has become associated mainly with moves towards the religious life. But there are five features that distinguish a vocation, and I see them as bringing people into the field of therapy with the positive sense of direction and dedication, hope and faith, which has often been more characteristic of religious life-choices.

The five features that, together, characterize a vocation are giftedness, belief in the power of the unconscious (indeed, in the unconscious itself), strength of purpose, reparativeness, and curiosity. With reference to curiosity, I would say that, as with all epistemological drives, the knowledge sought needs to be deep and detailed. It is not satisfying otherwise (nor will superficial acquaintance prove beneficial to our patients). The search is hardly ever satisfied anyway, or, at least, not for long. This makes our job all the richer: one never comes to the end of *knowing* about other people. One can never sit back and say, "Ah, now I know what makes this person tick", let alone, "what makes *people* tick". The most we can say is: "I think I know something more than I did about why this person is as he is", or "behaved as she did in those particular circumstances".

Belief in the power of the unconscious is taken as a given among us; but I do not think it should be, at least about the world beyond our own. There are people, of whom Jean-Paul Sartre was

one, who deny the very existence of an unconscious mind, unbelievable as it may seem to us. I know at least two intelligent,
well-educated doctors who simply say that there is no such thing.
If we challenge them, or offer what seem to us to be incontrovert-
ible examples, they will say, "But that's not unconscious. It's
obvious." Psychosomatic symptoms are a good field for argument
on the matter. I can never decide whether such people (e.g. the
doctors who think the unconscious is "all obvious") are extraordinarily talented at reading the unconscious, and so think it is
self-evident (which they often are), or very obstinate and stupid!

The need and wish to make reparation is probably the feature
that, above all others, displays the object-related nature of the
therapeutic relationship most clearly, and also leads into the
countertransference. It is a complex state, which I hesitate to call
a drive, because of the special instinctual use of that term in
classical Freudian psychology. Nevertheless, a constancy of wish
and purpose, and a deeply unconscious origin, with, usually, a
conscious component, makes the idea of "drive" accurate for this
context in reference to reparativeness. I am not speaking of whatever fantasy it is that makes rather unsophisticated people say
innocently, often sweetly, that they "want to help people". Individuals with a strong reparative drive *do* want to help people; but
in my view this is, of all the vocational qualities, the one that most
urgently requires analysis before it is put into practice. This it
does not, by any means, always get. There is a double need here:
usually one can locate a somewhat pathologically narcissistic
element in it; and also, such people have very often undergone
severe trauma of their own, usually during childhood or adolescence, which frequently leaves unhealed wounds. (This is part of
my own personal motivation.)

The concept of the "wounded healer" has received a certain
amount of attention in our field; there is no final consensus as to
whether one *has* to be in some way wounded to make a good
healer, as some people would contend. Indeed, unless one's own
pathology has received adequate therapeutic attention, there can
be danger in it. One may continue to try to heal oneself by
continual projections into others, which may effectively obscure
the quite different traumas existing in them. Or one's own behaviour may be disturbed and wrongheaded, and result in damaging
acting-out with patients. Whether or not one believes that the

"wounded healer" brings a special sensitivity to psychotherapeutic work, what is of primary importance is that the case for some solid analytic treatment of would-be therapists is strengthened if they are themselves already wounded by life.

Giftedness is hard to define, and even harder to write about. We are in the borderlands of the invidious and the unspeakable here. It may be the crucial factor that decides whether a student is selected or whether a therapist is really good at the work. It is easier to recognize, during a careful assessment interview, than to describe. As a concept, between therapists, it is freely used, and, in my experience, no one ever stops and says: "What do you mean?" It is common currency, and its meaning is taken as read—perhaps because it is so hard to speak about in detail. However, one feature, I think, tends to distinguish it—although I would find it difficult to test out, as it brings into play the other quite difficult term, which we have touched on already and are examining; my impression is that people who are naturally gifted also experience a sense of vocation. I have observed, particularly in the United States, where the profession has always had more "respectability" than it has in Britain, that some prospective therapists are drawn to the fold by reason of the fact, not that they are gifted or have a sense of vocation, but that they can envisage a life in which they are respected and safe. The job is seen as not too challenging (although this is obviously a matter of personal opinion), not too publicly exposing of limitations in the practitioner, and financially secure though not wealth-making. This view of it may draw in from general practice and general psychiatry people who are unadventurous, sometimes anxious and often socially ill-at-ease. Whereas the gifted person, who may well have received earlier input from an appropriate culture, brings to the work creativity, imagination, adventurousness, curiosity, a strong reparative drive, and—as with any other art-form (which I believe good therapy to be)—an ingredient X, which permeates the whole and marks out the person who has an untaught talent for certain sorts of subjective interactions with a naturally therapeutic quality. The sense of vocation that these people discover in themselves *will persist*. After an awful, exhausting day in which they may have seen ten or twelve patients, all in various states of suffering, they know without any shadow of doubt that there is, nevertheless, nothing else they would rather be doing. Such people do not really have to choose or decide what to do with their lives; it is just a question of searching out the best way of receiving an appropriate training—or, to put it even more simply, the best way of getting going.

In good-enough circumstances, one enters a personal analytic therapy as part of this training, and a considerable amount of care will be taken to uncover the complex reasons underlying the wish to be a therapist, which, in the gifted, will amount to a sense of conviction and faith in the choice. During the course of therapy, some people experience changes in their sense of self. For example, even in people with a strong desire for the work, the reparative drive may be revealed as deeply mixed up with fantasy, and also much more narcissistic than it at first appears. Very occasionally a student in training may discover, as may an otherwise devoted religious, that he was mistaken about the vocation, and he may leave. No shame attaches to this, though sometimes it is felt by the ex-student, or by an ex-postulant, for a while. However, it is ameliorated by relief. Unless features such as pathological narcissism are available for mutative analysis, the wish to heal others will not be sustained, and it is as well to discover this probability in good time, before long and difficult treatment processes are undertaken by the new young therapist. As I indicated earlier, a strong root may be an unworked-through traumatic life event, and this urgently needs attention if it is to be a source of strength. A therapist, I repeat, should not be treating projected aspects of the still-suffering self; envy of the patient, for example, may enter the picture and could be a severe disturbance. This is not to say that a qualified therapist should never again experience neurotic symptoms or depression, so long as these are accessible to continuing self-analysis. One of the enjoyments of doing psychotherapy is the capacity to identify closely, if fleetingly, with one's patients over a whole range of emotional experiences; a person who has become too detached or has developed, for him, a necessary armour as a result of personal analysis, may be disabled in his sensitivity and empathy.

Finally, there is strength of purpose, the fifth of the qualities that I see as characterizing a vocation. I touched on it when I described the sense of vocation as itself persisting. But it is about more than that; it is one of the reasons for working out more clearly for oneself some, at least, of the answers to the main question. It is harder to nurture strength of purpose if one has no distinct idea about what on earth one is doing or why. However, this is not to say that we won't at times feel completely lost and in the dark, because we will. There is an old maxim that simply runs, "the cobbler sticks to his last", and as it is a bald statement without further explanation or dependent clauses, it is hard to see what it is saying, unless it is something about carving out one's own pathway, knowing what it is, and demonstrating tenacity in staying with it. In the field of analytic therapy, we undertake relationships with disturbed and unhappy people who are suffering in highly individual ways; no two ways are quite the same, thanks to the infinite variety of human nature. Here we see one of the main obstacles to carrying out controlled series of psychotherapy treatments, a task that is sometimes attempted in units that accept large numbers of patients, but one that is, to my mind, unsuccessful. Not only do all our patients and their forms of unhappiness differ individually, but therapists are markedly different from each other in ways that, in our field, have an effect on outcomes. Furthermore, I am sure everyone has the experience of not, in many ways, being reliably the same himself, from one therapy to another. Anybody with any experience knows that there are therapists who are more comfortable with some types of psychopathology than with others. Indeed, carrying out large numbers of assessments and then placing patients with appropriate therapists, as I did for many years, made it essential that I should know something about who likes working with what and who doesn't. Enjoying the diagnostic category involved makes for better therapy than discomfort, anxiety, and excessive effort.

We know, therefore, at the beginning of a new treatment, that we have a long period of work with this person ahead of us, whether we see the person once a week or five times [and what this means in itself—the frequency of sessions—is another large subject, one that I have also discussed in the book I mentioned (Coltart, 1993), under the general heading of "Psychotherapy versus Psychoanalysis"]. We need various qualities, such as faith—in ourselves, and in the process we help to create—patience, and, if we can manage to develop and work on it in ourselves, the capacity to love. I do not refer either to liking or to sentimental or erotic feelings here, but to a quality that it is perfectly possible to work on and nurture in ourselves, is capable of constant critical appraisal, but is fundamentally warmly and caringly disposed to the individuals whom we come to know in the most intimate detail. Together, these features, which ripen in ourselves as we grow older, combine to produce a steadfast trust in the therapeutic procedure and in the relatively very small group of individuals, which is all we can encompass in our working lives. It has been rightly said, and it repays frequent reflection, that it is impossible to get to know someone in the microscopically close way that we do and not to love him or her, in spite of all their human failings and unpleasantness; and thus we trust also in our own strength of purpose.

It is quite a task we encounter in our everyday working lives. Doing good analytic therapy with a disturbed and suffering person, in which our only instrument from moment to moment is ourselves, is *difficult*, and you should never let anyone tell you otherwise. Some will try—especially doctors and other personnel in different branches of medicine, or even psychiatry. There is no need to argue the point; in fact, it is a waste of time: "A man convinced against his will / Retains his old conviction still." There is certainly no need to adopt any quiet airs of martyrdom or suffering of your own, a temptation to which I have certainly seen colleagues succumb. Remember who got you into this in the first place! But if you are exhausted at the end of a long day, during which you sat perfectly still in your chair, apparently doing nothing other than speaking occasionally, take it seriously when I say that you need to attend with real care to rest, relaxation, and refreshment, wherever you personally find it. Don't let your devotion to the job become too contaminated by superego elements, and certainly don't let guilt percolate into any of your forms of relaxation and rest. If you have *some* vocational qualities—and everyone has *some*, I believe, else they would hardly be in the field—then remember that not only did you steer yourself into this extraordinary job, but you did it, and do it, because you really want to, and there is nothing else you would rather be doing. It is hugely important to remember that, eccentric as it may appear to many people, we *do* know why we are here. And we are lucky that things came together so that our choice to "be here" was a real possibility for us. We have the most interesting job in the world.

CHAPTER THREE

Two's company, three's a crowd

I n the Autumn of 1989, I started the Introductory Course offered by the Institute of Group Analysis; this consisted of a weekly lecture with some time for discussion after it, and a weekly experiential group of one-and-a-half hours. The Course lasted for a year, with three breaks, totalling eight weeks. I had wanted to do it for a long time, but it was only once I began to retire in stages that I could comfortably fit it into my timetable.

It is difficult now to recall what I had expected, especially as both forethought and imagination were streaked with loose ends of information, from being acquainted with group analysts or people who had been in group therapy, and from occasional reading long ago, such as Bion's *Experiences in Groups* (1961). This sort of information can cloud the scene without being of any value and, indeed, may serve to reinforce real ignorance in a particularly resistant sort of way. What I increasingly realize is just how much the whole experience taught me, and this is almost more true of subsequent reflection on it than of the so-called

---

This paper was first given at a Conference held by the Institute of Group Analysis in September 1991.

experiential time in the group itself. I say "so-called" not in a spirit of criticism, but because there are inevitably serious impediments to true group experience in such a course—for everybody and, in a way that I will describe, for me in particular. This is not to undermine the value I attach to the whole event; it is more to say that the experience was deeply affected by certain in-built aspects of it and by not only who but what I am.

First, there was the limitation set by the year itself. I think the group as a whole was aware of this throughout. It illustrated, more vividly than most life-events do, something of what T. S. Eliot must have meant when he opened the poem *East Coker* with the words: "In my beginning is my end . . ." Most of us were stimulated by the time the end came to want more, to have the experience of participating in a long or an open-ended group; two, or perhaps three, of the members put this into effect and subsequently applied for the training. I am not aware of any who joined a true patients' group; which brings me to the second unavoidable feature of *this* group: while theoretically it is open to anyone to apply to join the Introductory Course, in the nature of things it is mainly professional workers in allied fields who want to and who are prepared to undertake the time and money commitment. There was no member of our group, I think I am right in saying, who was simply the man in the street—for example, an architect or a writer or a chemist or a bus driver. That this must affect the style and content of the process, I have no doubt, and while I can imagine ways in which this might occur, I do not know for sure. I did not read anything up about it. I read very little, in fact, and will say something more about that later.

Thus we come to a more detailed view of what I meant when I said that who and what I am had peculiar effects on the experience for me—and I use the term "peculiar" advisedly, in both its senses: that is, I believe the specificity of some of the effects to have been peculiar to myself; and some of them were peculiar, that is to say, odd, in a way I could not have visualized beforehand. We can side-step for the moment who I am—my self; there may be peculiar things about me, but that my individual character affected my group experience was, of course, not peculiar to me. On the contrary, it is simply an example of what life is all about for everyone, all the time. But my being a psychoanalyst—of individuals, that is—as one of the major elements of my whole identity made it all strange, absorbing, and at times quite difficult. I understand that very few, if any, practising senior psychoanalysts have ever done the Introductory Course, so there was no one I could get hold of in order to compare notes, or mull over difficulties.

I decided that I would, insofar as I could, conceal this massive fact about me for as long as possible. My reasons for doing so felt strong and clear to me, and, oddly enough, Lionel Kreeger, the Director of the IGA with whom I discussed my wish to do the course, subsequently reinforced these reasons, quite indirectly and unaware of the effect he was having. I will describe how this happened in a moment. My strongest reason was the wish not to have a distorting and inevitably powerful effect on the group before I had even had a chance to be in it, as myself and without my professional badges on. It is no good trying to underplay one's awareness of the irrationally influential effect of saying one is a psychoanalyst: it is far worse than saying one is a psychotherapist, or psychiatrist, or even doctor, and they are bad enough, I've used them all. There is a number of predictable responses to the information, in which the common denominator is a mixture of keen interest and wary alarm; the most that can be said for the announcement, which I now try to avoid at all costs in most situations, is that it certainly does not produce that look of glazed boredom that one observes in response to the revealing of some other professions, such as insurance broker, company lawyer, or "something in the City". Not only do people often feel a sort of licence to be quite ill-mannered about what they think psychoanalysts do, but there is, to this day, a large amount of fantasy and rather old-fashioned prejudice attached to our job in the minds of even quite a sophisticated public. How Dr Kreeger confirmed this view later was by a letter to *The Times*. There was a correspondence drifting along about this very subject—people's reactions to the discovery of other people's work. He said he and his wife had been at some gathering, and the usual question had cropped up, with, I think, some attempt at a sketchy job description in his answer; a few minutes later his wife was asked by a young woman, in an anxious whisper: "Is he doing it now?" This excellent little story exemplifies very precisely the response of an extraordinary number of people: the main fantasy, expressed in different ways, is that our all-seeing X-ray eyes are ever at work, seeking out the darker sides of the people who surround us; considerable power is ascribed to us, of a rather magical and unpleasant sort. It has something primitive about it, reminiscent of tribes far from what is called civilization, who are said to refuse to have their photographs taken, for fear of being robbed of their souls. And I deliberately mentioned just now that even quite sophisticated people can react like this, because it was at the heart of what I did not want to do to my fellow group members. I did not think that their reaction would be at the extreme end of the spectrum, because the likelihood that they would be working in disciplines allied to my own would probably mitigate their anxieties; but that they could not help being made unnecessarily aware of me and of what I might be thinking seemed to me to be not even a question, but a fact—and I wished to avoid it at all costs. When I first went to talk about my plan to Lionel Kreeger, I even suggested that I should use a pseudonym! In retrospect, I can see that this revealed the depths of my ignorance; he, with his unfailing courtesy, tried to change his fleeting expression of horrified amusement into one of kindly interest; but he fairly easily persuaded me that I would feel even more awkward than was already possible if I tried to mask myself to this extent. What finally convinced me was my awareness, derived from actually being an analyst, that if one strays from the path of Truth, whatever experience one is engaged with becomes muddled and invalid. In fact, I find this a useful maxim for life as well as for work; sticking to the truth is just so much easier. Being economical with it, or avoiding some aspect of it, is a very different matter from substituting a lie. I did speedily realize that my two middle names, Elizabeth Cameron, which I had used before in one or two other situations, would only serve to depersonalize me in this one and seriously interfere with any truths I might hope to discover from my year with the group. I solved the problem at the very first group meeting, when we all said our names; for once, I blessed the current social custom of using first names straight away on introduction. My generation has not taken easily to this custom, which feels to us over-familiar; on occasion, when people, usually younger than I, call me Nina at the beginning of a consultation, I have been known to give a rather frosty response. I think my whole name might have rung some bells; so I was grateful for the custom which in other circumstances I did not care for. Several members seemed keen to tell us what they did, but I simply said I did not want to say what I did, I wanted my identity in the group to be free from the contaminating effect of a professional label. Some others felt the same, and this was easily accepted. I discovered only at the end of the year that in fact two members of my group had known all along, but had respected my reticence and kept it to themselves, even among themselves, for which I was extremely grateful.

One of the first things I began to learn in the group was directly linked to this. I suppose I knew it before, but an interesting feature of the group, I often noticed, was its power to magnify certain things, or show them up in high relief. I observed how very strongly some people identified with their professional selves, and how reluctant they were to let them drop away. There were one or two people who for months seemed only able to speak, or be, within these working selves, as if only they would make them audible or visible or real—to them, as well as to us, I suspect.

But any notion I might have had of freeing myself from the *effects* of being an analyst were rapidly dispelled. One of the things I had never realized nearly so strongly before was just how deep and in one's bones and blood are the theory and practice of many years of being a full-time psychoanalyst, and in this I include, for brevity's sake, doing more active, broad-spectrum psychotherapy for about a third of the time.

Curiously enough, by that coinciding of life's events which Jung calls "synchronicity", there was a paper by Dr Sam Stein in *The International Journal of Psycho-Analysis* early in 1991, when I was thinking about this subject, called "The Influence of Theory on the Psychoanalyst's Countertransference". Sam Stein is a wise, humorous South African who went to Australia many years ago and is the much-loved elder in the small society in Adelaide, where I met him in 1988. He has put "the psychoanalyst's countertransference" in the title because he is focusing on a simple but enormously important theoretical idea, namely that the countertransference is the analyst's creation—arising from who he is—and is not solely the patient's creation, by means of endless complex projective identifications. He speaks of the prolonged business of living one's whole life while also being an analyst, with the training behind one, and yet keeping up one's training by all the daily means at one's disposal—working with patients, reading, discussion, seminars, conferences, and self-analysis. As the main plank in his presentation, he quotes from a paper by Goldberg (1989) called "A Shared View of the World" and it says so clearly something I came to realize in the group that I shall quote it again here:

> The fundamental stance of the analyst . . . is governed by his analytic theory. Here is where analyst differs from patient, i.e. a given phenomenon such as a dream or a free association is necessarily seen in a different way, because all of our facts (and perceptions) are soaked in theory. We never see any part of the psyche, without a theory of the psyche, and thus analytic theories, whether articulated or not, distinguish analysts from all non-analysts . . .

Stein goes on from here to say that Goldberg's statement, though profound, does not go far enough; and here I quote Stein himself.

> . . . our emotions, as well as our facts, are soaked in theory. The analyst is sensitized, by his theory, to focus on interactions and material of a certain kind. His way of working soaks into *all* his responses . . .

And he does mean "all"—our whole way of being and thinking is coloured forevermore. Really, it begins to be no wonder that the general public reacts to us the way it does! All this speaks exactly to my year's experience in the group and to the title of this paper. To put it as simply and as emphatically as I may—by now I can in no way not be a psychoanalyst. And I would add that, since by definition that identity has been moulded by my training and then in the crucible of the consulting-room, always alone with one other person, then for me the experience of two people and no more is the primary one of my working, and, I would add, waking life, and any more begins at once to feel like a crowd.

This phenomenon, which I realized as clearly as this for the first time in over thirty years, did not at all detract from the enormous interest that the group held for me; but that it did present me with peculiar and specific tasks is beyond doubt.

For one thing, I am not sure that I am capable of being a "good group member"; I don't even know quite what that would be; but for me, though I was, of course, aware of certain "group feelings" and events, and these were fascinating, that room was always peopled with fifteen individuals, each in complex relationships with all the others, and it was thus that I mainly thought about them. I found it much harder to perceive signs of the phenomenon that I am sure an experienced group analyst sees everywhere, all the time—namely, the group operating as a group, an organism with a strong evolving character and unconscious life of its own.

For another thing, and for me, outstripping in importance all that I have said above, there was the problem of trying not to be, a lot of the time, what Sam Stein's paper defines so clearly as what I am—a psychoanalyst "soaked in theory". This was by no means at the same level of ignorant silliness as imagining I might call myself Elizabeth Cameron. It was much more to do with not wanting to contaminate the experience of being a group member by too much in the way of reading unconscious messages from the other individuals, of thinking interpretatively, etc.—everything that is implied by what Stein's paper said. Not to mention talking like an analyst. I could imagine only too vividly the pitfalls lying ahead if I were to comment on remarks, behaviour, reactions of my fellow members, in the way to which I was deeply accustomed, all day and every day in my professional life. For example, I saw that I could fall into competing with our group conductor, and I must confess that what I hope was a sensitive awareness to this possibility never left me throughout the year. I was also very identified, at least to begin with, with her experience of having me in the group. I thought this must be difficult for her, and months later she told me that it had been—although more in anxious fantasy than in fact.

Another tightrope loomed, and I was constantly aware of being on it. I say "another" because I wrote a paper about eight years ago, called "On the Tightrope", about the balancing acts we have to bring off as psychoanalysts in our daily practice. Some of them turned up again in the group, little changed; in the analyst's consulting-room, the major ones concern when to speak, at which level, how much, with what emphasis, and so on. One can fall one way or another, and in that paper I described different sorts of falls and what they can lead to. Exactly the same problems cropped up again, I realized, for me in the group. Here, I am not implying that if I am at a dinner party, I am always perceiving things with a beady analytic eye and coming out with heavy interpretations that bring a deadly pall of silence to the table, rather as the dreaded cartoon-type analyst might. I hope and think, in spite of all I have said above, that the persona of psycho-analyst is not so dominant that it rules my self-presentation exclusively throughout my social and emotional life. Here, I think, one is helped by something that I have always given thought to; this is to do with language. An analytic therapist should always make it a first and ongoing concern to try to speak with patients in ordinary language. There are always simpler ways of putting theory and concepts that we may express in technical language when we speak to colleagues at scientific meetings, where it is permissible, precise, and economical. Most of my closest friends, as it happens, are not psychoanalysts; many are not even "in the field", and they would not thank me for penetrating insights into their unconscious lives as my contribu-tion to our friendships. Some of them, perhaps the wisest and most "normal", never give a thought to their unconscious mental life; indeed, if asked, might doubt that they have one. Once, talking to a G.P. friend about a difficult patient of hers, I delivered myself of a weighty piece of helpful interpretation. There was a pause: "But that's obvious", she said, in a rather puzzled way.

However, the experiential group was unique. It was not an ordinary social gathering. It had some things in common with the psychoanalyst's setting: not many, but enough to be seductive to the analytical me—above all, that powerful invisible ingredient, the will to work, in a certain way; a way that can lead to an increase in self-knowledge and might be painful, but would only succeed if we stuck with the truth about ourselves so far as we could. The setting, and our will to work, were such that the theory and practice, which for about half my life had, in Stein's word, "soaked" me through and through, were operating in me, with that special readiness for a certain sort of perceiving and thinking, in its highest gear. There was little I could do about that—it would have been impoverishing to myself to suppress it; all I could do was not frame it into speech—or, at least, not the regular forms of speech that might be said to comprise my "tech-nique" or analytic style; that is to say, the way of speaking that is second nature to me in a clinical situation but which for me is usually in my own consulting-room.

I was helped in managing this, insofar as I succeeded (and only the group and the conductor could comment on that), by my very real desire to participate as an ordinary group member and receive the refreshing benefits of being a sort of patient. There was much rather grumbly discussion, incidentally, as time went by, about the uncertain nature of the group. By definition, it was "experiential"; but as what? It was not defined as a therapeutic group, nor was it a training group; each of those was probably closer to the other than to what we were. It was a question without an answer. We remained uncertain—and that was part of what we were. We had to make of it what we could. This I did not find so hard, in itself; I wanted to be whatever the term is for the person on the receiving end, while being aware that such a person has to *work* in all forms of analytic therapy, to contribute to what one receives. If that person is a "patient", then that was all right by me. Several group members demonstrated quite clearly, however, that it was not all right by them. But I am sure most psychoanalysts know what it is like to envy their patients at times; the majority of us do not return to analysis after we have finished our first, nor had I ever wanted to—in reality. One is there at last, on one's own, carrying out a uniquely odd job that is really only learned by doing it, and many of us, who have a true sense of vocation about this rather cloistered life, would not have it otherwise. There are, of course, occasional patches of anxiety or depression, and these can be worked through; but simply envying one's patient occasionally the chance to lie down and be listened to and cared for is a strong but fleeting fantasy; it does not signify a sustained wish or intention.

Here, the chance to be a sort of patient was a delight, and I wanted to suck as much juice from it as I could. The only approximate solution was a kind of internal split, and this worked, more or less. Splitting need not necessarily be either pathological or total. I regarded this as splitting in the service of the ego—of all the me, that is, who did not want to function professionally there. And certainly this me was richly fed; as, indeed, was my psychoanalyst self, but privately, inside my head. I realized how infrequently I had ever functioned as part of a group; this in itself is probably deeply connected with the choice of job in the first place, which, as I indicated above, can have a vocational quality to it. I am not exactly antisocial in the extreme sense of the word;

but I was never a joiner, and I am to this day amazed at the number of people who go back to reunions of their school, or college, or regiment, or training hospital; or even at the many occasions on which analysts themselves meet solely for social purposes. I realized that many analysts must suffer, in a way I never had, from the solitary nature of the job. There are always people available to organize these gatherings, and although I quite like running things and have had my share of it in the British Psycho-Analytical Society, I infinitely prefer them to be about current administrative or political procedures that need organizing for the immediate future, rather than for the sake of reminiscent nostalgia, or just cheery getting-together.

A particular phenomenon of the group, which I noticed occurring, bore a relationship to this, my own characteristic dislike of jolly social events of any kind. Our group conductor told us at the beginning that, although there were no specific rules, it was thought advisable not to meet outside, during the lifetime of the group. This presented me with no difficulty, but I did observe that as the months went by, a couple of small sub-groups formed who used to go off for a drink together when we closed at 7 p.m. I hope I don't sound like The Sneak of the Upper Fourth; I mention it because my refusal to join them was something I learned from—notably, that I tend, as I have often thought before, to quite an extreme degree of need for separateness or what has been critically called a sort of stand-offishness, which it is. I was profoundly interested in each of the individual group members, but I had no desire to get to know them better apart from their being-in-the-group, because it was as group members that they interested me, and they, after all, *were* my group experience. I am not proposing this behaviour as either better or worse than the desire to make new friends and extend shared experience, which is in any case largely a function of a younger age group.

I did slowly begin to get some feeling for how people are influenced by being in a group, as opposed to the, to me more familiar, ways of being in a one-to-one relationship. Certain rather caricatured stereotypes appeared quite rapidly, only to disappear again as the complexities of the group and of simply being human took over. I should insert here that one of the things that affected my role in the group was my age. Apart from any personal dilemmas I was having about trying to conceal too much manifestation of what I did as my work, I was older by far than most of the others, a sort of Granny Figure. I was in my early 60s at the time. There was only one other person even within hailing range, a man of about 50, who often saw himself as the group father, not to say leader; this quite quickly transformed him into another stereotype altogether, and to my intense interest, I watched him become a scapegoat. This is not a phenomenon that can actually occur in one-to-one psychoanalysis, except in fantasy, but in a group, of course, it is quite possible. People took against his assumption of authority in his self-appointed leader role, and for a while he was met with quite a solid wall of hostility. It was fascinating to watch him insightfully learning from this, with the result that within quite a short time his good-humoured climb-down and discovery of humility had quite changed the atmosphere and won him an affectionate regard.

There were glimpses, or more, of other characters; the baby, or the little girl, who did look startlingly young though she turned out to be—amazingly—44; for reasons known only to herself, she maintained the illusion by what she wore and how she presented herself. There was the flirt, and the sphinx, and the chronic sufferer, and the Earth Mother, and the jolly good fellow, and the wide boy, and the teacher's pet. These were my private names for them, of course; we all remained throughout the year on rather tentative, courteous terms with each other due to the indeterminate nature of who or what we were, by group definition or lack of it; and, of course, to the fact of the End being forever in sight. And anyway, all these little labels blurred and faded and changed as time went by. Except for the sphinx, that is: this person remained almost entirely silent week after week after week; when a few words were squeezed out, they were quite shrewd and enabling. But the prevailing silence never let up. This, by the way, is not a disguised way of presenting myself. Indeed, I became extremely annoyed with the ferocious ungiving of this member, and towards the end said so in an attenuated fashion. In spite of what I have said above about my sense of peculiar tasks on a peculiarly difficult tightrope, I participated in the group quite actively. I tried to do the balancing act between acute analytic understanding and just making fairly routine comments; I have always, in any case, been a sharp observer of human manners, and after a few weeks I felt fairly confident in joining easily in group discussions that usually flowed freely after some awkward, sticky starts. It was quite readily accepted that in my granny role I could make shrewd remarks as part of our discussions about particular group members; they were heard as the wisdom of age and of worldly experience, and I was pleased that nobody, at any point, seemed to feel that I was making interpretations, or accused me of being too "analytic" in what I said. I am sure I was protected partly because I was very alert to the danger, and partly through using ordinary, homespun language.

One of the things I truly learned about myself—which in a way was not new, but in another way was borne in on me with greater force than ever before—was how my running stream of inner commentary on people tended towards the critical, with intolerance at the extreme. I don't mean I voiced much, or any, of this, but I certainly noticed it, and what I learned more about was how moment-to-moment living is really pretty tough for many people much of the time, and, moreover, what an admirable job most of them are quietly making of it. If that is called becoming more humble, then that I certainly became. Psychoanalysts tend to forget how extremely cut off they are from anything resembling normal life, for eight to ten hours every day. It is the darker side of the great luxury of having time and space to work deeply with just a few people. In this respect, I think experienced group analysts see much more of the world than we do, and I quite envy that. Also, I think we forget what a damaged and pathological section of the population we see. And I have observed, as the years have gone by, that there is a tendency for older, successful analysts to become self-satisfied and opinionated, and at the same time rather arthritic, in their views; indeed, I had actually written about this, naturally making a rather smug exception of myself, on the shaky grounds that I had such a clear view of it in others that I must have overcome it in myself. This was probably unwise, but I hope that my genuine admiration for the way several of the group members really struggled with painful bits of themselves and coped with them has worked in me for the better. I am not including the sphinx among those people. That person made no effort at all, so far as I could see, to join in, or help other people in their struggles, which it seems to me must be one of the main things a group is for. But several others, as well as battling bravely on with their own problems, developed amazingly skilful means of giving real emotional assistance and support to their fellow-battlers. This, of course, is something that by definition cannot happen except in group work: the value both of being able to give and to receive this sort of understanding and real insight from one's peers is unique to group analysis. It is one of the main reasons why I might refer people for this sort of treatment after seeing them in the consultation practice. I found this phenomenon extremely impressive and often moving, and it added to the increase in genuine sympathy in myself for other people and thus reduced my tendency to be over-critical.

The thing I most constantly missed was the privileged opportunity offered by individual analysis to go ever deeper into the dark recesses of the psyche of another person, and to have the time to use to the hilt the most random-seeming free associations. There certainly developed an absorbing group phenomenon whereby practically everyone came individually to the fore and received detailed attention when their need was great; I noticed time and time again that it was as if the turn of X or Y had come round, and the group facilitated the use of that session by X or Y alone, or very nearly alone. But time and again I also had the frustrated sense of people having to stop too soon, for someone else, because their own need boiled up, taking over too soon, and it was at these times that I felt most keenly that three's a crowd, and that one of the great blessings of the psychoanalytic space is that space, and the time to enjoy it. There is also the unique luxury of having the dedicated attention of one's analyst devoted entirely to one's self.

I think it was directly related to my long experience of working alone with people that I felt an almost continuous sense of pressure in the group. By this I mean that I mostly felt the pressure as from fourteen other individuals, and I did not often get the sense of being able to change the focus of my attention, so that it would be on "the group" rather than on each individual. I don't mean that I was uncomfortable or unrelaxed; it was a question of focusing, and the way I do it naturally exerted a pressure in that particular context. I greatly enjoyed being able to see people's faces all the time, as the analytic style deprives us, by the use of the couch, of the continuous play of expression on the human face.

To return to the question of my age for a moment, and from that to a personal experience I had not expected, and indeed, did not become aware of for quite a long time. I have said I was far older than everyone else there, and that, of course, included the Group Conductor, a quiet, attractive woman whom I judged to be in her early 40s. When I say quiet, I include not only that she had a rather calm and peaceful air about her, but also that she was not dominating or intrusive in the group process. I think if she had been, I would have been hard put to it not to challenge her, certainly to develop something negative in my transference to her. Of course, I have no way of knowing if group analytic conductors are ever dominating or intrusive—perhaps they are not—but I cannot help feeling that, in the nature of things, some must be, or at least abrasive, or provocative. But ours was not; she was very attentive and containing to the group, and I felt that she followed the patterns of its intricate dance rather than leading. For quite some time I did not detect any particular signs of transference to her in myself at all; then one day I noticed that I was pleased and rather relieved for her when she said something shrewd, and I was amused at this, since it was also clear to me that she did not need me to be anxious on her behalf; I recognized an ancient feeling about my younger sister, who was a worry in her teens, doing something grown-up and admirable.

But some months further on, I had quite a shock: rather suddenly, I abreacted some buried feelings to an event that was traumatic and nearly fifty years old. It all started because there were some empty chairs, and quite intensive group talk focused on people who were absent or missing. I will not go into the trauma here, but I developed an anxiety attack, and for a while felt very helpless and overcome, and also violently angry with our group conductor, wanting her to help and feeling she, too, was "missing" this and failing me. The group, as it was capable of doing at times, rallied to what felt like a crisis and worked superbly to contain me and put me together again. I can still remember almost exactly who did and said what, and this, of course, included the group leader, who eventually made a couple of most incisive and relieving comments. As I recovered, and the group, with exquisite tact, went about its other business and left me to do so, while at the same time not making me feel abandoned, I began to see something. Far beneath my rather cool, apparently neutral response to the group leader, I had been building up a primitive and strong transference to a mother, who then suddenly disappeared—or seemed to. After I was able to let the anxiety attack happen, then be angry, and then rescued, I gained some valuable insight into something that had never before been accessible to me, in all these years—namely, the anger towards my mother, which had been locked inside the anxiety. This experience then left me, not only with an increased respect for the potential of the group process, but with an affectionate, somewhat daughterly, feeling towards our group leader, notwithstanding that I was old enough to be her mother. When I had thoroughly worked through and assimilated the emotion that had so unexpectedly arisen in me, I felt very lucky that my single year of group experience had provided me with such a happening and grateful to the group and our conductor in a way I would never have anticipated.

So far, I have said nothing about the large group, which took the place of the lectures for the last of the three terms. This consisted of all the people attending the course—that is, all the small-group members, together with all the Group Analytic Institute staff, i.e. the leaders of the small groups—about 150 people altogether. I found the whole experience baffling and tedious, and my impression was that most of the others did too. I saw how valuable it would have been if a little education could have been given to us at the beginning of that last term. Sometimes, especially when starting a psychotherapy with someone who is absolutely ignorant of any aspect of it, it is not only more humane, but it is infinitely economical, to educate the patient into some of our ways of speaking and thinking. There is no earthly reason why patients should somehow be expected not only to accept, but to participate in, an event that is deeply familiar to us only through years of training and experience. I felt the large-group experience was a flop and on the whole a waste of time, and I was, and still am, critical of the people who were supposed to be running it, whatever that meant. About once in every session, someone would crank themselves up and, with a visible and audible effort, say something like: "I don't understand what we're all supposed to be doing." There would then be a long silence, punctuated by rumbles of agreement with this view. Eventually one of the staff might say, "I wonder what you think about that?"—one of those ill-judged, pseudo-analytic responses that rightly make people new to analysis grit their teeth with frustration. And not only people new to analysis—long-in-the-tooth old practitioners like me, too. I did not contribute, because I was pretty sure I would give myself away if I did. I understand that some interest centres on large groups currently and much is being thought and written about them. But I never read the texts suggested to us, even on small groups. I had never intended to run a group, or "do" anything further about it, and I wanted the whole course to be as purely experiential as possible for me. I thought it would be only too easy to become a "student" again, as opposed to a "patient", and there would have been a certain appeal in that. Reading would certainly have added to the possibility of that happening, and I did not want it to. The whole experience was absorbing anyway, and I did not want it clothed in intellectualizing and theory. All the events and phenomena of that year were massively interesting to me, in all sorts of different ways, and I am tremendously glad I did it. Even the tedium of the large groups held its own sort of fascination: for example, I was interested in the acute anxiety that some members of my small group manifested during and immediately after the large group, particularly when they would say fiercely: "I *will* say something next week, I'll *make* myself do it." The importance of "saying something", no matter what, seemed to become paramount. It made me think of the new young corporal who was being trained by his Sergeant Major to give orders to the platoon. He got them to attention smartly enough, with arms presented, and he got them marching briskly along, with himself at the rear and his big, tough Sergeant Major marching watchfully and critically alongside. Unfortunately, the camp was on the coast, and they were marching briskly towards the cliff, which, from being distant, came ever nearer. The corporal gaped and stammered. But nothing came out. He had forgotten the command to make them stop. Eventually the Sergeant Major bellowed at him: "Well, go on, Jones—say something, even if it's only good-bye!"

CHAPTER FOUR

Handling the transference

So many developments in the study of transference and countertransference have occurred in the last half-century that it is sometimes forgotten how much we owe to Freud. I propose to consider the papers written between 1911 and 1915 and often referred to collectively as "The Technique Papers". I do not mean to go over them in detail—I would rather people read them time and again for themselves; they invariably come across as fresh, lively, and packed with helpful advice; and his formulations are equally valuable for the beginner and the experienced practitioner. I mean only to view them for what they have to tell us about the transference, its theory and use; the use of the countertransference was not yet developed, and its detailed study really post-dates Freud by many years. It is of course referred to by implication several times, but it was not really studied as a subject in its own right until Paula Heimann focused directly on it in a now-famous paper in 1950. While we are refreshing our memories of the Technique papers, I will add some

---

This paper was written for a seminar attended by all the students in training with the West Midlands Psychotherapy Institute, in 1993.

thoughts of my own on subsequent developments and personal experience.

The first paper is called "The Dynamics of Transference" (Freud, 1912b). It is worth adding here that I think this one should be read in conjunction with two of the *Introductory Lectures on Psycho-Analysis* (1916–17), Nos. XXVII and XXVIII, which Freud produced a little later, in 1916. There are some useful, connected passages in them. In "The Dynamics of Transference", Freud explicitly broaches, for the first time, his understanding that, from one's earliest years, there are stereotypical templates in every individual, created both by genetic structure and by primary experience, which will forever underpin one's erotic pattern. All individuals strive to satisfy certain instinctual needs, meet their own preconditions for falling in love, and, more or less unconsciously, organize the means by which they try to reach their own ends. Essentially, this pattern cannot be rooted out or radically changed; but—especially where certain elements of it may never have been satisfied by reality, or have been held up in the course of development or only experienced in fantasy—it can, through analysis of the transference, be modified, sometimes to a considerable extent.

In fact, patients who have never consciously experienced certain sorts of feeling—say, quirks or depths of being in love, or ways of reacting when they feel cared for, or angry and hostile and critical emotions towards their nearest and dearest—may be difficult to work with, because the defences are so strong; but they may also be rewarding. Once the analyst is sure of a piece of transference and has an understanding of its value and how it is manifesting, one can plug away at it patiently until the strangeness of it (to patients) is minimized and they have a good feeling of their whole range of emotional capacity being expanded by experiencing something new. But it should not be forced. One should never push something—even something one is sure of—in the transference until one senses that patients are on the very edge of being able to know it fully for themselves. We come to Freud's warnings about this in a later chapter, but I stress it here as it is such a common error of technique. There is a saying: "A man convinced against his will / Retains his old conviction still", and this is true of all analytic therapy. Furthermore, there is a common countertransference failing that goes with it; this concerns the sort of situation in which one may have been repeating an interpretation, perhaps in slightly varied ways, for many weeks or even months, encountering only resistance, or rejection, or ignoring of the therapist by the patient, until one day the patient tells the therapist this very piece of insight as if it is completely new, and has never been alluded to before, and furthermore is the patient's own discovery. And in a sense it *is* all those things. One should resist the temptation, if humanly possible, to say, in a peevish voice: "But I've been saying that for ages", or something similar. The practice of analytic therapy, far more than most professions—and more than any lay-person could believe—requires a real worked-through capacity to be humble and self-effacing. What matters is—has the *patient* truly grasped the insight? *Not* whether one was bright enough to have seen it long since. The art is to learn sharply and fully to rejoice in the steps forward a patient takes; this has to be one of the primary sources of gratification for an analytic therapist. And it is certainly not advisable to seek for gratification—the narcissistic one of being seen to be smart or intellectually several jumps ahead.

The individual erotic patterns, which Strachey translated from Freud's German as the person's "instinctual cathexes", are the source of transference. In analytic treatment, which exerts a negative pull on the patient through the direction of interpretations and the focusing of an intense beam of scrutiny on the patient's neuroses, the person of the therapist becomes increasingly important to the patient, and "finally every conflict has to be fought out in the sphere of transference". Here is one of the most important features of this first paper: clearly, at that time, transference tended to be thought of as if it were always positive, and this is a mistake that young therapists are still inclined to make today, probably because (whatever people may say about their technique) the all-important early stages of treatment do rather concentrate on building a good rapport and a solid therapeutic, or working, alliance; and it is, in fact, positive elements of *transference* that blend with hope and trust to create and maintain the alliance. In fact, there are some analysts, notably Kleinians, who maintain that the concept of the "therapeutic alliance", and any theory that may derive from it, are superfluous to our needs, as it is all transference, and should be treated as such. A Day Symposium organized by the British Society a few years ago made this very clear. Freud stresses here, not only that the genetic roots of affection and sympathy are always, if traced right back, sexual in origin (by his definition, that is), but also that negative elements of transference, which lead to conflict and therefore to resistance, are *always* found side by side with the more socially acceptable, more easily accessible positive ones. Freud *for the first time* here introduces the actual term "Ambivalence".

Also *for the first time* in this paper Freud refers to what is now called "The Golden Rule". He is describing how the transference becomes, for the patient, such a genuine affective experience that fantasy turns into real longing and recovery of memory into acting-out or -in. In other words, the transference is the source, not only of pleasant cooperation, but also of strong resistance, so that the patient begins "to disregard the fundamental rules of psychoanalysis". The patient ceases to be frank and open and becomes secretive and withholding, or passionate and angrily demanding. He/she may seem to be a bit mad temporarily, or at least very different from the agreeable and compliant creature we knew at the beginning of treatment. Thus, through the transference work, the core of the neurosis is gradually revealed, and "it is on this field—of the phenomenon of transference—that the victory (that is the cure of the neurosis) must be won". Freud ends the paper engagingly by reminding us that such transference work is *extremely difficult*. We have been stuck, in the dark, trying to exercise negative capability as creatively as possible, and have thought: "Oh, if only I could see the transference." And when one *does*, it is as if a light had begun to shine on the hitherto baffling situations. Freud adds—and we soon begin to recognize this for ourselves—that it carries the greatest conviction to the patient, and hence to us as we do it.

In the paper called "On Beginning the Treatment", Freud (1913c) is at pains to demonstrate that, in a neurotic patient, transference will always develop: the therapist does not have to assist it by any particular efforts; so long as we instruct the patient about free associations—i.e. the golden rule—it will unfold of itself, and the "delicate procedure", as Freud calls it, will continue unaided until it encounters a resistance. Sometimes this will take quite a long time. But there is also a type of patient who almost at once will open by announcing that he/she has nothing to say. Freud handles this, in the first instance, by instructing the patient—yet again—in the fundamental rule. We have to remember that he was didactic by nature and still had a greater faith, not only in education, but in being obeyed, than we might have today. But he also indicates that transference is *already in existence*, stating that a strong transference resistance has already come to the fore in order to defend the neurosis. This, he implies, he would tackle, after encouraging the golden rule, by transference interpretation, if he possibly could; he insists that if "the patient looks into his mind again, then early transference signals will appear".

However, the most usual primary task is "attaching the patient to the person of the doctor in order to establish" what Freud calls "effective transference", and on the whole he advises that this sort of interpretation should not begin until a strong rapport exists. By this, we would now realize that he is referring to the treatment alliance. One further quotation at this point: "To ensure a strong attachment, nothing need be done but giving the patient time. If one exhibits a serious interest in him, carefully clears away the resistances that crop up at the beginning and avoids making certain mistakes, he will of himself form such an attachment; and will link the doctor up with one of the imagos of the people by whom he was accustomed to be treated with affection." He adds that one should not moralize, fling diagnoses at him, make clever lightning guesses when the patient is nowhere near ready for them, nor use intellectual reasoning, which will all fall on deaf ears. These, I think, would be what he meant by "certain mistakes".

It is important to try to remember, while reading these papers, that psychoanalysis was still tremendously NEW: I believe it is almost impossible for us to imagine fully that for a therapist to sit behind a patient, restraining himself from diagnosing or being clever or putting forward his own personality—even from talking at all for long periods—was not only revolutionary and amazing, but quite alarming, especially when practically the only person writing about it was listened to, and faithfully copied by, those who were interested or were struggling to do it. Freud himself used his written papers to work things out as he went along, which accounts for certain self-contradictions that crop up (and which I think deserve admiration rather than criticism, which has lately become fashionable). To this day, there are two large categories of patients from whom Freud was probably gathering most of the material on which he based his ideas on transference: those who are extremely anxious and need quite a lot of careful work, with some informed guessing at transference colouring, before they can settle into treatment; and, at the other extreme, those—often hysterics, of whom Freud saw far more, and more florid examples, than we do now—who come in to treatment with what is called a "readiness for transference", or even with a fantasy-laden transference thoroughly established, based perhaps only on a short preliminary interview or even purely on imagination. It is important not to leave this uninterpreted, but to welcome it and begin to work with it straight away.

I would like to insert here, in this chapter on handling the transference, something about which I have always felt strongly, and which I have learned more about from doing clinical seminars with many generations of students. It is a matter on which there are quite sharply divided opinions, certainly within the British Society; I have encountered arguments when teaching abroad, but views are less definite, for example in the United States. The subject whether—or not—to take a history during the preliminary interview. My view is as follows: If one is sent a patient by an assessor who has taken a good history and made notes about it, it is valuable to ask to see those notes and to memorize a considerable amount of the history before one starts the treatment. *Or*, in one's own preliminary interview with a prospective patient, some detailed history should be taken by oneself. Or both. It is essential, I believe, for the smooth development and effective handling of the transference, that the therapist has a firm grasp on the patient's view of the main object-relationships of his/her early life—and by that I mean up to late adolescence, not just the first two or three years. If one is going to understand the individual transference, rather than impose a theoretical structure on it—which is then inevitably similar for everyone—one needs to know a lot about what it was like to have been the patient as a child, the details of the relationships to his/her mother, father, siblings, or their surrogates—whoever played important influential roles in the development. Interpretations that allude to recognizable nuances of what the patient's own life was like—such as, "You are feeling anxious and lonely the way you did when you were left alone in the house with both your parents out at work", or "You seem to have the same jealous feelings about the next patient as you did about your little brother"—carry more weight and are therefore more effective agents for insight and change, than are more theoretical part-object interpretations that have no particular meaning to *this* patient.

A clinical seminar in which some of the students have no knowledge of the personal history of their own patients and rely entirely on theoretical transference work from the beginning can be, in my experience, a lamentable event. I recall one in which it became clear to me, while listening to several sessions of a particular patient's material, that the patient's mother *must* have abandoned him, suddenly, and probably through dying, at an early age. I asked the student. She did not know; she did not even know whether the patient's mother was alive or dead *now*, or, if dead, when. She was not skilled yet in handling transference, and the session she presented was literally embarrassing, as she came out with ill-digested theory and tried to push it into the unhappy and bewildered patient. This is one of the points I want to stress; a very experienced analyst can handle a patient's offerings entirely in the here and now of the transference with a skill and sensitivity that can make the reporting of a session a convincing pleasure to listen to. A student or an inexperienced (or even simply a not very good) analyst cannot. It takes years of experience to train the third ear, the intuition, the sum-total of all the analytic skills, in fact, to carry out this most delicate task. I believe the sort of clumsy ineptitude that I have often heard from beginners trained in the school of thought that ascribes all value to early theory and fantasy, and none to the individual and his history, can do real psychic harm to patients. Also, when we consider the vast amount of work that has been done on details of child development, with, in relation to the example I have given, special reference to parental loss in childhood—I think we may at least understand why I consider this point important, and why I am stressing that each patient is a human being with a highly personalized history, and that it is our job to treat this with respect and understanding; we must therefore be familiar with the details of the history, and we must use it.

There is one more thing to be said about the 1913 paper, "On Beginning the Treatment", viewing it from where we can elicit information about transference. Right at the end, Freud rather tantalizingly refers to the phenomenon of "transference cure", really only to say that it can happen but that it will not last. "Transference cure", which many people will not have seen, is an odd and usually temporary mixture of the cheering effects of very positive transference, with an underpinning of strong resistance. In other words, a patient is so energized and perked up by the beneficent effects of being in love with a reliable parental figure (only he or she probably would not see it like that) that the symptoms vanish, and the patient may leave the treatment prematurely, assuring the therapist and themselves—and others—that everything in the garden is now lovely. Freud states fairly categorically that it will not last, and I think this may be linked with the extreme nature of some of the hysterical symptoms, including conversions, that he encountered. The resistance, in this phenomenon, consists in the splitting, the denial of the negative and the ignoring of the self-deception; and in taking the slightly manic state to be true happiness. An apparent change from a symptom such as a conversion, which has been fed by a lot of psychic energy—if it is not worked through and thoroughly understood—simply squashes the pathological structure, splits off and temporarily represses it, but does not eliminate it; and the energy, or distorted libido, forces its way out somewhere else pretty soon in the shape of another symptom. The patient is then disappointed and angry and probably blames psychoanalysis and the therapist, who may him/herself have used a lot of energy to try, fruitlessly, to stop the patient leaving. Having said that, it is important to add that we now know that, just occasionally, "transference cure" *does* last. Perhaps it was not a "transference cure" at all—the label may be a misnomer. But a patient who quite rapidly forms a largely positive, loving, idealizing relationship with the therapist *may* thus mobilize energies that have simply been untapped for years, and the self-image may, as a result, improve so greatly that real ego expansion occurs, and the patient conceivably begins to build creatively on this and to maintain the core of the improvement thus initiated. Certain religious conversions show this persistence, and I have seen it in at least three patients, who were followed up—without interpretation!

One of these patients was a really ghastly late-middle-aged woman sent to me for assessment and referral (to see if I thought therapy possible), by her G.P., who was at his wits' end. The woman was known in his practice as Miss Heartsink. She wasn't exactly a hypochondriac—she was not on a grand-enough scale for that. True hypochondriasis is a serious diagnosis of a usually monosymptomatic paranoid psychosis and is in fact quite rare. But she was what gets *called* a hypochondriac. Spinsterish (the feminist side of me is reluctant to use this adjective, but the sad fact remains that, politically incorrect as it may be, it does still convey a wealth of meaning), somewhat paranoid, obsessional, priggish as they often are (and which shows their narcissistic contempt for the inept doctors), she visited the surgery regularly with a succession of shifting, indecisive symptoms on which she dwelt with fanatical intensity while they lasted and did not seem to notice when they changed. The gratification obtained from them remained constant. The G.P., an excellent one, was kind but tough with this lady; and also, thinking she might well be presenting an involutional depression, quite properly treated her with three courses of different anti-depressants, none of which helped at all. The patient was a late Catholic convert and was attached in some way to a convent of Dominican nuns, who also got a lot of her complaints and dependence. She did a humble job and often went off sick. I saw her four times as a sort of extended consultation-cum-brief-therapy. I did not do anything much. She was totally *un*psychologically minded, and a few attempts at interpretation from me met with complete incomprehension. I thought she was quite unsuitable to refer on for therapy. But she fell in love with me. In a quiet, devoted, fortunately un-clingy way, she unconsciously arranged to channel all her frustrated libido onto me—fixated, as it was, at a homosexual, primitive level, on an early imago of a long-dead mother. This was twenty years ago. She changed massively and has maintained the change. She stopped "doctoring" and instead took up voluntary work—again in a humble capacity—with a Catholic orphans' charity. She writes to me—neat, quite humorous little letters, about three times a year. I always write back to her. Now the food is the right food, she seems able to subsist on remarkably small quantities of it. She is one of the proofs to me that what I believe to be "transference cure" does exist and can last. She also proves to me something I have long believed and sometimes written and spoken about: that it is healthier and more beneficial to the whole system to love rather than to *be* loved. There is a potent myth to the contrary, but this way of looking at it is true nevertheless and can be tested by long-term observation.

Back to Freud: there were two papers in 1914. The title of the first, "Remembering, Repeating and Working Through" (1914g), tells us a good deal. The paper is one of my favourites, because Freud is very self-revealing in it, in a way that shows us a kind, and almost tender, aspect of himself, which is an unusual view of the didactic, patriarchal genius. The emphasis throughout could have lengthened the title somewhat and made it even more accurate. Freud is concentrating on remembering, repeating, and working through *in the transference*. He is pointing out that even in insightful patients, repressed emotions and early experiences incapable of coming straight into memory may appear as transference feelings and behaviour that then enable the analyst to make accurate translations and thus broaden the self-experience of the patient. Christopher Bollas later wrote about this in his excellent first book, *The Shadow of the Object* (1987). Here Freud introduces the concept of the "compulsion to repeat", which is so clearly demonstrated in people's erotic patterns, and which we must know from ourselves as well as from studying patients.

In this connection, there is a particular quotation from the paper, which reminds us that it was written about fifty years before Winnicott brought in his notion of the "need to play". Freud says:

> We admit the compulsion to repeat harmlessly into the transference as a playground in which it is allowed to expand in almost complete freedom; thus we give the symptoms a new transference meaning and create the transference neurosis.

The transference neurosis is to this day extremely important, and technically it is where most of the effective transference work takes place: it is an intermediate region between the incomprehensible neurotic illness and real life—most often it has an unpleasantness and tension to it, which removes the early happy basking in positive transference, and it is much more accessible to interpretation, and is ultimately more easily resolved, than straight positive or negative transference. It is focused entirely on the therapist.

This is where the young therapist really learns to develop patient endurance and negative capability; the transference neurosis may be, in a sense, an artificial *illness*, partly created by human nature and partly by the interpretative guiding skill of the analyst. But patients have to become conversant with their own resistances and their need to go on repeating; and time is required before working-through is completed, and, almost in defiance of the patients' wish to keep something alive and real— as it seems, and *is* to them—they also have to go on siding with the analyst's therapeutic work if they are honest and if they can, and stick to the golden rule. It is only gradually that patients become convinced that, for example, fierce anger, red-hot jealousy, sexual longing, and so forth are no longer directed at their true (i.e. original) object, but at the analyst, and that the analyst is an inappropriate object; then the patients can slowly put such feelings in their true perspective and leave them behind in their own emotional histories where they belong. In a nutshell, this is really the aim of an analytic therapy. Economical, pointed interpretations, often repeated times without number until a true light of insight finally dawns, are the order of the day here. There is nothing to be alarmed about when a florid transference neurosis appears. It is a gift to be worked with. Young therapists do sometimes feel frightened at the strength of the emotional turmoil they have unleashed; here it is important to remember, and to cultivate faith, that the *analytic process is trustworthy*. Skilful interpretation is required, of course, especially in the case of a heatedly erotized transference; it may be a good idea to obtain some supervision for a while to assist the process.

Freud continues with this subject in another paper, which is called "Observations on Transference Love" (1915a [1914]). Freud thought this was the best of them, and certainly it has life and vigour to it. It is in this paper that Freud delivers himself of his warning, which remains as vital to take in and learn today as ever it was then: "The analyst must recognize that the patient's falling in love with him is induced by the analytic situation and *is not to be attributed to the charms of his own person*" (my italics). How often have I heard therapists who should know better, as well as inexperienced ones and students, describing the passionate positive transference of a patient in a complacent, slightly fatuous way, sucking narcissistic juice from it, which yet again makes one realize that the therapist has fallen into the old error that Freud was so caustically warning against—namely, that the patient loves him because he is loveable, or admires her because she is admirable. It is nothing of the sort. It is transference.

Some of Freud's best metaphors appear in this paper—for example:

> The patient loses all understanding of "transference' for a while; it is as though a piece of make-believe had been stopped by the sudden irruption of reality—as when, for instance, a cry of FIRE is raised during a theatrical performance.

Effectively, this loss of grip by the patient constitutes a resistance to treatment—the flowing continuum of interpretative therapy is interrupted by the patient's protest that he really is in love with the analyst, or really does need to be in touch at weekends, or really has ceased to trust and admire the analyst because he has seen through him; the variations are infinite. Another excellent metaphor comes into view as Freud deals with the difficult tasks that face the analyst, especially if the analyst personally loses grip and starts to share the illusion, or gets very anxious. Freud is saying that all phenomena must be accepted, as when the tone of the whole transference relationship was more muted and amiable; he is warning against trying to turn off the patient's intensity by any means whatsoever:

> To urge the patient to suppress, renounce or sublimate her instincts the moment she has admitted her erotic transference would be, not an analytic way of dealing with them, but a senseless one. It would be just as though, after summoning up a spirit from the underworld by cunning spells, one were to send him down again without having asked him a single question. One would have brought the Repressed into consciousness, only to repress it once more in fright. The patient would feel humiliated and would take revenge.

Nor does Freud advocate a middle course, such as guiding the relationship into calmer channels or raising it to a higher intellectual level. Always Freud returns to the baseline—that it is *dangerous* (his word) to depart from the foundation of psycho-analysis, which is *truthfulness:* we must take what comes, and sit it out.

Here he moves on to another famous, and still completely applicable, piece of teaching. If anyone thinks this is old-fashioned or out of date, then further reflection is required. Analytic therapy must be carried out in abstinence. One has only to know the analytic world well and keep up with the ethico-legal history of our movement to realize that, even more today than in 1914, Freud is right to use the word "danger". In the whole known world of analytic therapy, there are about 100 cases that *come to light*, every two years or so, of analysts and therapists who, probably, have sexual affairs with their patients. Some appear to get away with it—for some reason, *marrying* the patient gives it a cloak of respectability, though the marriages are unlikely to last. Sometimes this problem presents chronic headaches to analytic societies, who may know and yet have to *not know* what is happening, lacking proof, or, frequently, lacking the bold mouse who would volunteer to bell the cat. Gossip may spread information, but making good use of it is extremely tricky and difficult. I think a piece of useful advice is that it is better not to gossip at all if it can be avoided; but analytic societies, perhaps because of the extremes of confidentiality and aloneness necessary in the work, seem to be peculiarly liable to become hothouses for gossip about each other.

Here I would attempt to consolidate the importance of Freud's view by adding that our fundamental ethic can be summed up in one sentence: patients are vulnerable, and under no circumstances whatsoever should we exploit, or act out with them, financially, practically, emotionally, or sexually. Talents for self-deception, so common in human nature, do not exclude analytic therapists. Let us return to Freud, whose compelling clarity of thought and style is unbeatable (the patient under discussion is female):

> It is a fundamental principle that the patient's need and longing be allowed to persist in her as long as is necessary, in order that they may serve as forces impelling her to do work and to make changes; and that we must beware of appeasing those forces by means of surrogates; and anything we could offer would be surrogate because, until her repressions are

removed, she is incapable of getting real satisfaction. Acting-out of any description by the analyst even with the highest aims would only achieve the patient's neurotic aims, and *never* the analyst's therapeutic aims. It is disastrous for the analysis, and the patient, if her erotic transference needs are met; she will be acting out what she ought only to have remembered and kept within the sphere of psychical events.

And one may add that it is the analyst's task to see to it that it is kept within the sphere of psychical events. Freud, then, with great skill, elucidates that there is no model in real life for what analytic therapists actually have to do; they have to let it be quietly but constantly known to the patient, by their whole manner, that while they can take and work with anything the patient manifests, they are also "proof against any temptation" as they gradually trace the maybe violently passionate transference back to its unconscious origins and bring it slowly into consciousness by means of consistent interpretation. We have to demonstrate, slowly, that there are no new elements in this current love, or hate, but that it is entirely composed of repetitive patterns, which, slowly, come to seem incongruous in the here and now and are mainly from childhood in origin. Thus we aim to uncover the patient's infantile object choice, the preconditions the patient sets upon gratification, and the often intricate fantasies woven around it. This is the undoing of the neurosis.

Freud, with his usual honesty, does point out at the end of this paper that we cannot truly say that this analytic in-loveness is "not real"—it is sometimes shatteringly real for the patient. All we can do is hone our language skilfully so that we work on the incongruity of it rather than the unreality. Freud says that, in any case, the state of being in love, wherever it happens, is more abnormal than normal, and in another paper—"On Narcissism" (1914c)—he compares it to a kind of lunacy. But it is certainly isolated and intensified in analytic therapy by the very special attention paid to it, and it is on its lack of regard for reality that any attempt at a real relationship that may evolve out of it founders. The patient's state of transference demands can never be gratified; the analyst who sets up a real-life relationship with the patient is not only sharing a delusion but has allowed his/her narcissism to rule the day, believing that he/she can match the fantasy. Omnipotence says that it can make it work this time;

real-life testing says it cannot. This brave and excellent and, in the context of its time, quite startling paper of Freud's is a warning that there can be real dangers in the handling of transference. If ever one is in doubt about one's own responses or course of action, some supervision, or even one discussion, with a senior analyst whom one trusts and who is generally known through the network of analysts as having integrity and having no shadowy gossip attached to his or her name is an excellent plan.

If the doubt is primarily about one's technique, and one is uncomfortably aware that one does not know how to handle the kinds of interpretation that are waiting to be made, a useful technical hint is as follows: when an erotic, passionate, or very intense emotional transference is in evidence in the here and now, one can, without suppressing the material or warning the patient off, take the interpretations *backward in time*. An attempt should be made to pick up some historical patterning that is recognizable—for example, a reference may be made to a powerful person in the past who has been important in this aspect of the patient's love relationships; an appropriate "genetic" interpretation may be constructed. This will re-focus the patient, who is still, in spite of the resistance of the current strong feelings for the analyst, probably trying to work; it will temporarily introduce a longitudinal theme-note even to a patient who is completely caught up in the transference neurosis and has ceased to acknowledge it for what it is. If, on the other hand (and this is very different from the erotic situation), the patient seems very stuck in the past, perseverating about a hated figure of childhood and unable to leave a preoccupation with a really unhappy, deprived, traumatized period of his/her life, the transference work may be brought *forward in time* into the here and now; the therapist should try to get in on the act somehow, even if only by the simple device of saying something like: "I believe you're very anxious about whether I could hurt you like that"—or—"about getting so upset and angry with me", and sticking with the manoeuvre in spite of protests.

In the *Introductory Lectures* (XXVII and XXVIII), Freud (1916–17) makes a few remarks about suggestion. A critic who is hostile may say: But surely you are simply operating on suggestion and hypnotizing the patient. Suggestion inevitably is theoretical; the moment a therapeutic intervention begins to be personalized, directly connected up with an event or an emotional situation in the patient's life, it is becoming an interpretation—or at least, a technically permissible comment—and is not a suggestion at all. Furthermore, one cannot "suggest" a memory, especially of an aggressive or erotic impulse, or an experience; one would be doing wild analysis; that field is wide open to the analyst's fantasy. And although there is much to be said for letting our own fantasies run free in our own minds while we are receiving patients' communications—in the same open free-associative state that we enjoin on them—this is quite different from letting fantasy rule our attempts at interpretation.

Suggestion only produces a combination of intellectual theorizing and fantasy, whereas interpretation gets down to the nuts and bolts of an individual's psychic structure. Interpretation goes far deeper, because it is accurately aimed; it opens out conflict areas and brings the unconscious nearer to consciousness. Thus it produces movement in the therapy, whereas suggestion does not; suggestion only blurs things, covers up, and, in fact, reinforces resistance. This is partly because it is instantly recognizable. It is hard to demonstrate this by example, but if one catches oneself doing it, one will know at once, and so will patients. They may continue to listen, but they will, especially if they are psychologically minded, give it the scant respect it deserves and temporarily be shaken in their reliance on the analyst. The same goes for interventions that are too vague and generalized.

Finally, and logically here, it seems important to add something about Strachey's famous remark, in his 1934 paper, that "only the transference interpretation is mutative". Sometimes I think it is a pity that this statement was ever made; it sort of hypnotizes people, especially young analysts at the beginning of their careers, and it gets linked up with the superego. Beginners get anxious if they find they cannot by any means construct a transference interpretation and have not yet developed the verbal knack of making an appropriate transference interpretation out of practically anything or nothing. This is a skill to be learned, but it is not an easy one, and meanwhile Strachey's dictum hangs about accusingly on the edges of the therapeutic situation. What is hardly ever recalled is what the rest of Strachey's paper is about: that is, the *need for, and value of, extra-transference interpretations!* He uses a metaphor to the effect that most of the daily work we do is in the realm of comment, clarification, and extra-transference interpretation. This he compares to a body of soldiers making their plans, covering the ground, clearing away obstacles—until, finally, as a result of all these preparatory moves, the enemy outpost itself yields and is taken. This is the moment of the effective transference interpretation. A considerable amount of any patient's material presents opportunities for telling extra-transference interpretations, and it is a great pity to waste it, or distort it out of all recognition in order to drag it into the transference. The classic example is when one has one spouse of a warring couple in treatment: one will hear, in the patient's accounts of the latest battle, references that show his own patterns and echoes of his early relationships, and he is going to be much more struck if one can point this out clearly than if one makes a slavish attempt to produce a clumsy transference interpretation of a "you-mean-me" type; it may, just, be a valid attempt, but more likely it will sound idiotic, as there are no accessible levels at all at which the patient *does* mean you. He is talking about his wife, and he needs as much help as he can get with that, by your shining a torch into the recesses of what is affecting his emotions and behaviour *there*. He may also have a dominant neurotic pattern, of which the marital conflict is only a part, and the opportunities for the transference approach lie in one's long-term tackling of that.

There is always stimulation and refreshment in returning to papers of Freud's, and I hope that these reflections on re-reading what Freud was writing about, eighty years ago, may assist in reminding us what an enjoyable and worthwhile undertaking such re-visiting is.

CHAPTER FIVE

A philosopher and his mind

I n 1967, a man was referred to me by a colleague for five-times-a-week psychoanalysis. I will give the first paragraph of the notes of my consultation with him exactly as I wrote it then; it still seems as vivid a picture of the man I slowly came to know so well as I would ever have written at any point since:

> An eccentric individual. He arrived sweating, smelly, untidy and slightly late, and launched descriptively into his recent psychiatric life, with many strange grimaces and odd tremors in his voice, betraying, I suppose, anxiety. His long grey hair floated randomly about his face and head. One might have guessed his occupation from his appearance and manner; he is a University Reader in Philosophy.

For some reason, and very unusually for me—I think because I continually found him so intractable and so strange—I kept notes on the analysis, a few lines per session, for almost the whole of the six years he was with me. It was an extraordinary event to read through this man's whole analysis; the notes included a number of letters from him, once when he worked at an

American University for six months, and once when he ruptured his Achilles tendon and had to be in hospital for a few weeks. The reading took about eight hours altogether. The atmosphere of the analysis was strongly conveyed; sometimes I experienced a distinctly claustrophobic sense of it, which I did then remember feeling during individual sessions. Constant obsessional ruminations about his sleep pattern (insomnia was his main presenting symptom), exact details of his medication, and minute particulars of how he felt, psychically and physically, all combined to exert a monotonous, grinding pressure on me, the implicit—and sometimes explicit—message being: "Do something." But the message contained a deadly double-bind, to which I shall return.

Careful study of the notes on the consultation, or preliminary session, reveals (as it so often does) a great deal of information and material of potential significance about this eccentric and deeply neurotic man. He had recently terminated, against the analyst's advice, nine years of twice-weekly therapy with a male analyst considerably older than himself. He complained of three main things in respect of that treatment. He lay on the couch, and he always felt deprived of contact and response. He said he would get so frustrated that he "felt like kicking Dr X"—but added: "Of course, I'm a coward about anger; I can't express it, though that's nothing to do with politeness." He added firmly that he was not going to lie on the couch here; unless he could see me, he was going elsewhere, until he found an analyst who allowed it. I did not feel strongly about the point, as it happened, and I agreed that he should sit up.

Then he said there had been no transference work in his previous treatment, and he regarded that as a real failure. Of course he belonged to an intellectual class that knew a great deal about psychoanalysis, its theory and techniques. Furthermore, he had had earlier encounters with it in his life. I must admit that he seemed to offer plenty of material appropriate to transference work, and this was proved to be the case during analysis, although using it with a sense of authentic encounter was more problematical.

Finally, he complained that Dr X had "generously offered" prescriptions for any amount of whatever drug he, the patient, wanted. This was typical of what turned out to be a knack, in the patient, for the ambivalent double-binding of others; I have no doubt he twisted Dr X's arm to prescribe for him in a way his own G.P. refused to do. Then he complained that Dr X gave him far too much (by what he considered normal standards; he himself wanted it). And he also expressed distaste for being able to control him so easily. It was a lesson in the unwisdom of being particularly "kind" to patients, I thought. The drugs referred to were sedatives and hypnotics, with the occasional anti-depressant thrown in.

He told me quite a lot about his family and early life, with a certain practised fluency. He was 43 at this point and was the younger by four years of two brothers. He did not like, or enjoy the company of, his brother, who was married with two teenage children. His father was a Ukrainian Jew, "an intellectual who failed to be a genius, and wanted me to be one instead; by now he is 75, a clown and a sneerer". His mother, then also 75, was "a dominating, powerful, cold and imperceptive woman, with strong, imposing views". The patient said, with concentrated venom: "I hate her more than anyone in the world." Nevertheless, he visited the parents every Sunday. I should add here that he lived alone, and although he was mean in his attitudes to other people, his own apartment was very expensive. He had been greatly favouritized as a child, over the brother. He had idealized his father until his teens, he said, but, more importantly, he had realized that both parents had idealized *him*, sharing their hope and ambition—and, for a long time, belief—that he was a genius. He made it clear that he had been idealized because of the entertaining brilliance of his mind and speech, his quaint perceptions, and his amusing and penetrating comments on life—all this from a very young age. He went to a special school run by a Kleinian analyst called Susan Isaacs, who had since written a book based on the school, called *Intellectual Growth of Young Children* (1930). In this book, the patient was frequently quoted verbatim, and he brought it to show me. I made it clear that it sufficed for him to tell me about it. He added: "But I am not a genius." There was an extraordinary quality to this remark; on the one hand, it was said in such a way as to suggest there might be room for doubt; on the other, there was a pathetic and sad resignation about it.

With a certain boldness arising out of giving this self-picture, the patient, whom I will call John, told me (a) that he required me to be very intelligent, (b) that he expected to be given extra time if he needed it—"as Dr X always had", and (c) that he expected me to medicate him according to his own demands. I responded briskly that there would be *no question* of either (b) or (c) and that I supposed (a) would be revealed, or not, soon enough. He put his head on one side and gave a strange smile and grimace; I read it as partly annoyed and partly relieved.

The sessions began the following week. The early ones were devoted to trying to impress me with the quality of his mind, which rapidly began to feel to me as if it should have a capital M. He also spent time demonstrating to me how much he already understood about his psychopathology and striving to block any possible entry of mine by formulating psychoanalytic insights, mingled with philosophical language. In a disaffected way, he related various sexual fantasies to me, featuring sado-masochism. He explained to me that he "tended to a Berkeleian view of absence"! Fortunately I knew a couple of limericks, which I thought summarized adequately such knowledge of Berkeley as I might need.

1. *There was a young man who said: "God*
Must think it exceedingly odd
That this old oak-tree
Continues to be,
When there's no-one about in the quad.

2. *Dear Sir: Your astonishment's odd;*
I am always about in the quad,
And that's why this tree
Continues to be
Observed by yours faithfully, God.

I did not quote these limericks to John, partly because I imagined that he knew them already. Nor did I ever just accept statements of his that were clothed in philosophical concepts, but would ask him to explain what he meant in ordinary language. I thought that accepting them as if I understood them (even when I did) would be colluding with him in a game that would make us seem specially clever and would separate us in a conspiratorial union above the mass of lesser brains who were comparatively stupid or ill-educated.

He told me, when speaking of his parents, that his mother was "very keen that he should get better"—a remark that was later revealed as containing violent and vengeful fantasy on his part. It was also connected with the double-bind on me, to which I said I would return, and I will now describe it. He had to appear, and I thought that this was consciously true, as if he wanted to "get better" himself—else why was he here? And would I expend any effort on him if he did not want to, or even if he was ambivalent? Yet at the same time, in wishing to be better, he was aligning himself entirely with his mother and the conscious manifestation of *her* wish; this was anathema to him. His symptoms, particularly his chronic insomnia and his social unease, were also his powerful weapons in his lifelong vengeful battle with her; and furthermore, the transference to me was, as a direct result of this double-bind, extremely conflictual. It seems almost strange to me now, but early on in his analysis none of this was conscious to him; and it was only through minutely detailed dissection of the transference that it all became clearer, and the connections were made between his hatred of his mother, the use of his disturbances as a weapon, and the negative undercurrents in the transference. He had said he wanted transference work, but when it came, he did not like it, and he resisted it strongly; he had probably done so with some success in his previous therapy, and I surmised that then it was also much more opaque with a male analyst, and perhaps less intense.

This work also led into an exploration of one of his ways of relating to his mind as an object. A deeper conflict than that which had thus far coloured the transference to me lay in a fixation to a development stage when (using Kohutian theory here) he had been at his most narcissistically grandiose—particularly in his expectations that the precocious power of his mind was sufficient to conquer anyone, whatever the subject under discussion. By "conquer" it transpired that he meant that significant adults would, if there were arguments or attempts to control, or even teach him, quite rapidly give in to his way of seeing something, or his wish to do something, with apparent admiration and a meaningful exchange of glances (which he would watch for), as if to say, or so he thought: "Of course he's right—he's so clever we must yield to his judgement, he knows best." I imagine, if glances were exchanged, it was more likely that they were accompanied by a resigned sigh and a view that although he was "adorable" because of his precocity, his will had become so strong (i.e. they had already "spoiled" him so much) that it was more than they cared to do to embark on a prolonged battle with him. The deep conflict in his relationship to his mind at this stage, when he was about 3, therefore consisted in a persistent grandiose conviction that he was truly omnipotent, which, however was chronically contaminated, or so it felt to him, by a recognition that he was not. He did not trust the admiring love of his internalized objects, because he had also correctly perceived in their "giving in" to him a weary anger, an impatience, a withdrawal of love, a coldness, and an absolutely certain knowledge that if they could trouble to exert themselves, they could overrule his stubborn precocity. He therefore, in his final, and most unconscious self-awareness, did not trust his parents' love for him *nor* the power of his mind; and this was deeply distressing and depressing. One could, with some accuracy, say that they practised a sort of double-bind on him—that is, under their submissive, but genuine, admiration they were also angry, critical, and anxious about him. He had become profoundly conditioned to believing he was loved and cared for only *on account of* his brilliance and the subtle and amazing thoughts and words his mind was capable of. He had no hope at all that if he was silly and naughty, or, worse, infantile, full of rage and tantrums, and "boring" (a terrible label of contempt and dismissiveness from both his parents), he would be loved, looked after, and forgiven just the same, He would therefore desperately redouble his efforts to exert omnipotence, and in so doing, I guessed, though he did not say, become more obnoxious and isolated; and this behaviour had persisted until the time when I came to know him.

Most of this, I can deduce from my notes, was worked on endlessly and thoroughly, usually clothed in classical theory and language, which was nearly all that was available, at least to me, at the time. The result often seems to me now to be clumsy and my interpretations not "experience-near", as Kohut would say. It is much easier now to formulate ideas about John's very early life than it was then. But with the help of the transference and faithfully following its guidance, and the early writings of Winnicott, it seems that quite a lot of what was really important about him and where and why he was stuck did get conveyed. Nevertheless, I do ask myself, during this recent perusal, whether, had I had the richness of such writings as those of Khan, Kohut, and

Bollas available to me then, I could have analysed this man's inmost conditions and suffering with more skill and truth and reached him more fully.

I should like to consider for a moment the way in which Winnicott's concepts of True Self/False Self applied to this patient. Certainly a large proportion of his analysis was concerned with working on the sort of thing that these ideas summarized. Aphoristically, I could say of the psychopathology of the patient: "His mind ruined his life." It is probably accurate to say that in some people extreme self-consciousness accompanies—or is even a synonym for—the False Self. Furthermore, the self-conscious mind is the creator and organizer of the False Self. To be watched, ideally, in fantasy, with loving admiration was such an important condition of John's early precocity that he was controllingly identified with the Watcher, and in adult life he could not escape from the split and the subsequent state of mind that this implies. Of course, we all, to some degree, create, and live conventionally in the world, through a False Self; the True Self, in essence, is, as Lacan (1977) points out, truly unconscious, made up of the elements of primary process, random and strong. But it is the source of all energy, and "genuine" people show in expressive living that they are much more in touch with this source. If we define the True Self as capable of originating natural, spontaneous, "first-hand" emotion and behaviour, then we are bound to see that John's self-experience and self-description was undoubtedly that of a False Self. He felt incapable of the sort of genuineness and cathexis of objects that he thought, rightly, was implied by "natural" and "spontaneous". He was almost perpetually conscious of the splits whereby he was the Watcher of his mind, and the performer, and the organizer. The performance, tragically, was of "*living*". On one occasion, he cried, in a way that was for a moment an expression of authentic anguish: "I've forgotten how to act myself"—not even ". . . be myself", but, such was his parlous and despairing state, ". . . *act* myself". John wrote a lot of poetry and sometimes quoted it to me. One of his poems, which had real feeling in it, began: "The tragedy fell flat . . ." It went on to reveal that, after all, there was no audience—the actor was alone.

It was, he knew, his mind that betrayed him; it seemingly had a Midas touch. The story of King Midas, who wished for the ability to turn things that he touched into gold and had his wish granted, is one of grimness and horror, leading only to death. In John's case, if ever he "forgot himself" for a few moments and expressed, even *experienced*, a true first-hand emotion, his mind would instantly be back on duty, watching and dehumanizing his self. And yet it was this mind that he also continued to idealize, admire, rely on, and use in his "precocious" attempts to seduce and impress the world. One of his gifts—and it was extraordinary—was a memory-store of long poems and huge quantities of Shakespeare; any poem or passage that took his fancy could be absorbed in a relatively short time and quoted on the slightest appropriate occasion. I thought that the sense of disappearing inside the thoughts and language of another must be a rest from the ever-vigilant, exhausting job of living his own life, in an apparently sane way, from morning till night.

Night, of course, would relentlessly come, and with it John's major presenting symptom: insomnia. If there was one thing that John apparently wanted to "get better" more than anything else, it was his insomnia. Everybody who knew John at all well, and above all his parents, were aware of him being insomniac. He treated passing social enquiries as to how he was as questions about how he was sleeping. He very speedily took to giving me a detailed report on the previous night as an introduction to every session. John lived alone, but every Sunday, as I mentioned earlier, he visited his parents for tea; he hated his mother and disliked and despised his father, but he was still attached, dependent, and vengeful. He would say he went out of duty and because they were elderly and they wanted him, but this shallow bluff did not deceive even him, although to begin with he denied his dependency and the other reason that I thought was paramount. This was to demonstrate regularly to them that he was *not* "getting better" and so carry on his vengeful war of attrition. His mother made it clear that it would bring her real happiness if John could convey news of peaceful sleep; she rightly saw that this would entail much else—reduction in anxieties, increase in enjoyment of life. So this, with stubborn grimness and at deep and lasting cost to his well-being, John refused to provide. It is a bitter affliction in life to use oneself as one's weapon in an ongoing war whose origins are lost in time and irretrievable by memory.

I will not go into the details of his insomnia; suffice it to say that he very rarely had a night of "natural" sleep; he took vast quantities of mixed medicaments, sometimes 12–15 tablets a night, and had various doctors and doctor–friends contributing to his stores, all unbeknown to each other. It is of greater interest in this context to try to see how his mind treated "sleeping" as its own primary and singular object; sleep itself had become an impossibly idealized state whose secret function, among others, was to disappoint him and let him down, as did he and his mind to anyone who had high hopes of it and him. Similarities with how he had experienced his parents, especially his mother, as he grew up, were also evident. The insomnia had that particular resistance to analysis that is characteristic of a symptom that is, by definition, always outside the range of direct transference analysis. We were always talking *about* it, rather than it informing our talk. Gradually it became clearer how over-determined it was, which again increased its resistant power; like the many-headed hydra, it could flourish to fight another day, even when one of its meanings could be so extensively understood that it might have lost strength through familiarity, if not through mutative interpretation.

Paradoxically, although he felt he ought to be able to "think himself" asleep, sleep was dreaded as a loss of control by mind. John believed, in a way and obstinately against much evidence to the contrary, that he had such control over his self in everyday life, but even though his mind would work ingeniously at ways of trying to get him to sleep, it seemed that the sense of escape into the unknown made these efforts ultimately and paradoxically frightening. It was as if he might disappear and never come back. In spite of a fascinated and serious preoccupation with suicide and death as the only answer to his existential problems, it seemed that there was not an exact parallel between death and sleep, which remained an object of dread in a way that death did not. Sleep represented a merging with mother and a loss of self; this meaning came up in connection with associations to the story of Hansel and Gretel. John did have a genuine intellectual curiosity, and he could understand how the children were driven forward by a similar curiosity into the depths of the wood and then led to trying to eat bits of the sugar-and-gingerbread house;

but this brought the terrifying old witch, who said she would eat *them*. In spite of the fact that John had a fantasy that he would have been saved by what Kohut calls the "merger transference", he was far too wary and self-conscious to let it come about. He was, unconsciously, too afraid that I would eat him.

Sleep also, to John's controlling mind, stood for something that he ought to be able to *learn* how to do. But there was a severe and early fracture in his ability to learn, which forever after contaminated the process. During the early stages of learning— and this went right back to his first days at school when he was a precocious 3-year-old—he was found to be exceptionally bright. For a short while, he would learn with ease—English, French, Latin, Mathematics. Then, rather suddenly, he would become less achieving; his unusual capacities seemed to fade; and thereafter they never regained their starry quality, although new subjects produced the same phenomenon and then followed the same downhill curve. Apart from his remarkable "learning by heart" of poetry and drama, learning anything was a struggle and a disappointment to him all through his life. He *was* very intelligent, and his learning was still at a higher level than most people's, but he always found it hard and was always dismissive of what he could do when compared to what he dimly hoped for. For example, he got a First in Philosophy, but was at a University where sometimes "Starred Firsts" were given, and of course that was what he should have had. Sleep became, as it were, a Starred First. Furthermore, the complication of a sour envy of those few who could and did do better than he came into the picture and made his own experience of learning more fraught and unhappy. I concluded that John was a person "wrecked by success" (Freud). A perpetuation of his brilliant learning level would have represented the final failure of his secret hope that he could be loved for himself alone, his greedy, smelly, infantile self, and not for his miraculous mind.

A word about dreams: Whether it was a function of his high levels of self-observing consciousness to keep dreams at bay, I could never decide. But John dreamed very rarely, and when he did, the amount of secondary process elaboration they received on their journey from him to me was such that I hardly ever felt a sense of conviction when trying to create some interpretation.

One way and another, through experience, I realized that the whole business of sleep had to be crept up on from some unexpected quarter, so that John and his mind were, so to speak, tricked into a yielding of his addiction to insomnia. After about three years of analysis, when his ability to express emotion as part of a conscious fantasy was more genuine, I began to notice that if he could express aggressive feeling *at* me, he slept better for several nights. At first his ways of doing it were tentative and indirect. For example, I observed, after some long time, that there could occur a deadly monotony in certain series of sessions, which I experienced as pressurizing, aggressive, and difficult to bear. He would go on and on about what I have noted as "a dreary, heavy, sadistically coloured sequence of breasts, sleep, shit—breasts, sleep, shit"! I would interpret the low-grade continuous level of attack, and he might then step it up a bit; if I could only *help* him to do something to get *over* his obsessional thinking, then he might be able to *stop*, but I *wanted* his thoughts as they *came*, didn't I? In such ways he often tried to expose and shame me for not being "as good at my work as I thought I was" and for my self-satisfaction in the very presence of my deficiency and inadequacy.

From the rather anal fixation level of some of his thinking, he suffered quite markedly from shame, or the anticipation of shame, especially socially, and he tried all sorts of ways of displacing this into me. However, although he would sleep better, he found this aggressive behaviour in himself quite difficult to tolerate, for a long time, though it gradually became more fluent; it caused him to fall in his own grandiose self-esteem (one of his delusional self-attitudes), and he felt he could only be raised again if I not only made it clear that I cared uniquely for him, but also that I forgave him for what he had done (and wanted to do) to me. When I would not, but described what he was up to, made a transference interpretation, or remained silent, he became frantic and demanding and then elaborated a fantasy of blissful reconciliation and reunion, in which he tended and cared for my injuries—caused by him, of course. This is a particular slant that I have almost always come across in people who use sado-masochism as characterological behaviour. In turn the images of reconciliation would be followed by quite viciously sadistic fantasy, which had then to be expiated, often by increase in anxieties and return to insomnia, in order that I might be protected, especially during my holidays. He suffered over separations and dreaded them, telling me he wanted me not to enjoy my times away from him. It was very noticeable that, although this rise in the levels of contact with his true self, and aggression, was exactly accompanied by better sleep on less medication, he never acknowledged the part that analysis (thus, I) had played in bringing about the improvement.

For a long time I could not decide whether this inability to acknowledge me was due to splitting and what Bion has called attacks on linking, or whether it was his envious meanness. On reflection, now, I would say it was undoubtedly both. Unless his own narcissism was being regularly fed by a relationship (other than with me, of course), he could be so hurtfully grudging that I realized it was a form of sadism. An example of him being "permitted" to be generous was during a glamorous relationship he had for a couple of years with a famous American star of stage and screen, who genuinely seemed to have fallen heavily for him; he could not speak highly enough of all her near-perfect attributes. He did, by the way, have a surprising number of sexual affairs in his life, and a proportion of the women stayed loyal to him and enabled him to develop the nearest he could come to friendship. I say "surprising" because to me he seemed peculiarly unattractive in all sorts of ways, including sexually; he was quite good-looking but he grimaced, and groaned, and cracked his knuckles much of the time. Also, as with many deeply neurotic people, his skin was greyish and very slightly damp (I could see a sort of glisten on it), and I well recall the wettish flabby handshake when I first met him. He was what the Buddhists would call *akusala*—"unwholesome"! And, as I indicated right at the beginning, he smelt. This continued, strong and offensive, until I could bring myself to begin to interpret it as part of his message to me and the world; I pointed out that it was not only actively aggressive, but also it said: "I am uncared for." The smelling improved, but I never developed warmth towards him or, as I discussed in several papers in my first book, *Slouching towards Bethlehem* (Coltart, 1992b), the special kind of love that is such a regular feature of our particular long, deep intimacy with most of our patients. And I do not think this absence was simply due

to him not being "my type", or anything banal of that nature.
I believe it said something about a crippling deficiency in his
mother's early pre-verbal relationship to him and to his true self,
and projectively I became the cold and critical, unloving, "bad"
mother. Insofar as this was countertransference, which I liked to
believe at least some of it was, it was quite a difficult one to
handle.

Finally, there was another feature of the analysis, which I
gradually realized was capable of releasing him from his mind's
torment, which kept him awake while it tried to force him to
sleep. This was a certain sort of discussion about suicide. He had,
several times in his life—the first at age 14, come closer than do
most people to realizing recurring fantasies of suicide. I remember being considerably helped by the writings of Winnicott and of
Guntrip when I was working with John. He was deeply capable of
what Winnicott called "the fear of annihilation", and yet he could,
paradoxically, think about creating his own annihilation, largely
because to control himself and his mind and its fears was a
dominant wish with him. I did not consider that he had already
brought about his own inner psychic death long ago, as Guntrip
describes in some of the most deadly, empty, schizoid patients.
John had plenty of real anxieties and hidden true feelings. But he
was afraid of the strength of these. Where I felt Guntrip (1968)
had accurately divined part of John's existential anguish was in
what he called "the tragic self-contradictoriness in the problem
of schizoid suicide". He adds: "The longing to die represents the
schizoid need to withdraw the ego from a world that is too
much for it to cope with. All available energy goes into a quiet but
tenacious determination to fade into oblivion by means of gas,
hypnotic pills or drowning." On each occasion—five in all—John
had been what he called "saved" (which was his more rational ego
speaking) by becoming hypomanic. It was quite clear from his
description of the emotional state that had supervened to deflect
him that it was certainly hypomania. Eventually there was one
occurrence during the analysis, the only occasion when I had
become seriously concerned about him and allowed him to ring
me during a weekend; it was precipitated by a firm and quite
unexpected rejection from the glamorous film star. I welcomed
the hypomania then as much as he did, and of course it enabled
him to become very aggressive towards me, which was most

valuable; and also to be truly witty for a change. He regarded himself as a sophisticated wit in any case, and he was often pained and angry when I did not respond to his rather laboured and, to me, unfunny humour. I would have shown it if I had appreciated it, though as I was quite near the beginning of my career as an analyst, I doubt whether I would have laughed in the uninhibited way that I find so easy at this end of my professional life.

The sort of discussion that initiated sleep rather than insomnia was one in which he would find that a truer self became accessible, as he hesitantly tried to explore the inner meanings of the dangerously real attraction that suicide held for him. It seemed, firstly, that there *was*, alongside what I said earlier, a simple, genuinely felt equation between death and sleep. He could enter a near-delusional state in which he had but to will the end and provide the means, and he would, after all, be able to induce peaceful sleep by this act of will (mind). When he swung up into the rescuing hypomanic state, he would accuse himself violently of "lunatic bloody nonsense". If we did not reach the necessary level of deep and concentrated attention in our talk about it, he would feel shame and fear about various aspects of what he thought; he feared being accused of "boasting", for a start. He *was* a boastful man, and he knew it, and it caused him considerable anguish. Then he feared being mocked and humiliated instead of being understood. He feared being told he "didn't mean it", that his fantasies were shallow and unreal, and, with the part of him in which this was also true, he felt ashamed. These scornful and humiliating attacks all derived from a powerful internal figure that bore considerable resemblance to, and was, indeed, based on, the true selves of his parents in their cold and bored relationship to him. (Ultimately, of course, their derisive belittling served to protect *them* from the narcissistic attack on them represented by his suicidal thoughts.) But he could eventually get deeper inside himself and, as it were, bypass this figure, and then we could, through our close empathic attention, relieve him of his torment and insomnia. Insofar as he had also experienced a good side to his mother, which belonged rather to his middle childhood than to his infancy, he had reinforced it with wishful ideas, and it was with this figure that he sought the prototypical reconciliation that he sometimes tried to effect with me. Above all, in death he longed for such a reunion, and in his nearest approaches to suicide he believed that he would find it and, with it, rest and peace and bliss.

The analysis of John and his mind proceeded thus for six years, and then we began to think about stopping, for in many ways he had made real improvements, not least in somewhat better sleep and in the experiencing of a more natural and unforced access to true self elements. He expressed himself as "about as satisfied as I'm ever likely to be, and you know what a critical bugger I am". Of course, we could have done more. One often feels that, and I believe it is right that one should; but I felt it more strongly with him than with many patients. At least I could be aware that in feeling inclined to stop he was not necessarily striving to please me, which had frequently been one of his modes of being in the analysis. He thoroughly understood by then the entrapping double-bind of wanting to be better because the other person wanted and needed it (which brought huge resistance into his own drive to health). He had tried to ensure that my narcissism did not receive much gratification from any of the distinct improvements he knew about. He still called the cheque he gave me each month "your unearned income"! His leaving was markedly eased in any case by our agreed decision that he should have some group analysis; we had discussed this at length and eventually, with his agreement, I had referred him to a friend of mine, the Director of the Group Analytic Practice, who had offered him a place in a group he ran for "mature people with social difficulties". John left analysis in mid-1973.

Four years later, he wrote me a brief note, enclosing a small cheque for a charity I was connected with, saying simply that he had seen that they were mounting an appeal, and he would like to contribute. I wrote a note to thank him; I remember that I thought about the appeal, to *him*, of "an appeal" for a kind of help. Five days later, I had a letter from a friend and colleague of his at the University, who said that I might not have heard that he had died; what she could not know was that it was on the day after he sent the cheque and the anniversary of the day he had left analysis. She added: "Apparently it was his own decision." So his mind, the spoiler of his life, won in the end; it seemed he had not sufficiently internalized my therapeutic value to him in my absence. He must have felt very confident that I would come to know of his death and the date on which he arranged it, for I imagine the date was entirely and consciously a last attacking signal to me. And, indeed, alongside the letter, the next day there was a notice in *The Times*, which he knew I read. It was not just a death announcement; it was a paragraph about him and his work (he had written two books on philosophical subjects) and was perfectly obvious on the last page. He must have known that an obituary was prepared, as the subjects of them are consulted when they are written. I was sorry that he was not there to see it in print; it is a true mark of specialness and esteem to get an obituary in *The Times*, and his narcissism would have relished it. He left no notes for anyone and, knowing the temptation that writing a note would have offered to his verbosity and his histrionic talent, I admired the dignity and forbearance of his silent departure.

CHAPTER SIX

Blood, shit, and tears:
a case of ulcerative colitis
treated by psychoanalysis

Starting almost exactly twenty-six years ago, I treated a patient with severe ulcerative colitis for three years in full psychoanalysis. I kept very detailed notes and wrote up virtually every session; this was one of the ways in which I handled psychopathology, which was quite new to me (and I still do, on occasion). I became extremely interested in psychosomatic illness, of which ulcerative colitis is one of the "Big Seven".[1] Obviously I must have thought I might write about that patient sometime, because in 1969, towards the end of the three years, I asked the Royal Society of Medicine, of which I was then a member, to prepare a bibliographical list for me. An outstanding feature of this list today is what is *not* on it, and how short it is. As a result of combing the American and the British literature, the librarian produced only 31 references to ulcerative colitis, and that included three separate papers by Engel (e.g. 1954, 1967) and three by Melitta Sperling (e.g. 1957). There were no hypotheses either of ulcerative colitis or of psychosomatic illness

---

[1] The others are peptic ulcer, hypertension, asthma, rheumatoid arthritis, eczema, and anorexia nervosa.

over-all; the general interest that has produced extensive work on psychosomatic illness is a product of the last twenty years.

But to me the most significant factor now is that there was, as yet, no rich background of *coherent* theory or technique on object-relations, self-psychology, or narcissistic character disorder, all of which would have provided a different climate in which to study this patient. References were so randomly scattered, when present at all in the literature, that they were difficult to assemble or see how they would eventually fit into a full-bodied theory. The notion of "the mysterious leap from the mind to the body" was prominent, whereas only ten years later Murray Jackson could write, in a paper entitled "The Mind–Body Frontier—the Problem of the Mysterious Leap":[2]

> "Somatization" and "conversion" are useful and necessary clinical categories; both types of symptoms may at times appear with startling suddenness, giving the appearance of "a leap" . . . But the real leap lies in the mind of the observer, who jumps from one conceptual frame to another, an exhausting and confusing activity.

These conceptual frames included the physiological, the neuro-biological, ideas on symbol formation and primary fantasy, ideas on the *absence* of symbol formation and fantasy, the theory of hysterical conversion, the theory of "primordial speechlessness" or preoedipal conversion, and views on the purely psychogenic causality of somatization.

If you imagine the confusion that all this represented to the mind of a young analyst in the early years of private practice and link it to the minimal and scattered information I have mentioned—on theories of object-relations, the self, and narcissism—you can perhaps imagine also that I experienced alternating frustration and amazement as I ploughed my way through all those careful notes: frustration at what I had not known and could not think or say, and amazement at how constantly lively, nevertheless, the therapeutic dialogue was between us. Before I tell his story, I will discuss briefly the sorts of ideas I *was* using.

---

[2] A paper read to the Psychiatric Section of the Royal Society of Medicine in 1978, a copy of which they gave me; later printed, so far as I know, only in the *Bulletin of the British Psychoanalytical Society*.

I do have to add, however (and I think this is often true when we look back on accounts of analyses from many years ago, either our own or other people's), that I am not by any means convinced that the outcome would have been all that different from the patient's point of view had I had access to all the literature that has appeared since 1969. Psychoanalysis is such a powerful and mysterious instrument that it is my impression that the patients who were destined to improve—or indeed deteriorate—under its impact would be likely to do so today, much as they would have fifty years ago, for all that we may pride ourselves on our advanced sophistication in theory and technique. This may be a humbling thought, or it may be a thought that many do not agree with; but I believe it to be true, and it is true largely on account of the "Ingredient X" that exists between analyst and patient in a long analytic treatment.

One feature that I think was *better* then, in the literature, than it tends to be now was the descriptive phenomenology of psychosomatic illness: such authors as Sperling (1957), Engel and Schmale (1967; Schmale, 1958, 1964), and Alexander (1950), did not pretend to be fully understanding of the aetiology, that is, they knew they were not *explaining* it, in all they wrote, but some of their detailed case histories are beautiful pieces of work. Through the 1950s and the 1960s, ulcerative colitis patients received special attention from such workers as Wittkower (1938, 1967), Feldman, Engel (1954, 1967), Paulley (1964), Lindemann, Wolff, and Sperling (1957), and, apart from Sperling—who always tended towards the dogmatic—their descriptions of what they understood, what they did, and why, in the setting of detailed case studies, are tentative but vivid. The same goes for some of these physicians, and others, working with cases of asthma, peptic ulceration, migraine, and eczema; and I particularly enjoyed the papers on anorexia nervosa by A. H. Crisp (1963, 1966, 1968), a general psychiatrist sympathetic to psychoanalysis, at Guys Hospital. Some people—for example, Alexander (1950), and the Paris school, culminating in the work of Marty, Fain, David, and de M'uzan—saw patients with a wide range of symptoms categorized as psychosomatic and, using analytic principles, carried out research interviews, or brief psychotherapy, in order to try to expand their theory of how these extraordinary illnesses came into being and were maintained, sometimes with remissions, over many years.

One of the main areas of interest, from the beginning, was the making of a clear distinction between conversion hysteria and psychosomatic symptomatology. It was thought that in the conversion hysterias—that is, genuine neuroses—the soma translates an unconscious wish of the psyche, expressed symbolically in an unconscious fantasy; the patient presents a true symptom, often out of the blue, and often, once cured, by hypnosis or interpretation, never to be repeated; the body has lent itself and its functioning to the mind to use in its service, usually to remove the self, or defend it, from a stress situation. In psychosomatic illness, then and now seen as more primitive and more mysterious, the body *seemed to do its own thinking*. The patient suffered from an organic disorder, with demonstrable physiological dysfunction and often extensive tissue changes of which he was unaware, and the illness, which would recur—and could be disabling to the point of death—seemed, in a way that was at once obvious *and* mysterious, to be linked with the patient's personality and life-history. The physical findings were defined mainly as signs rather than symptoms.[3] Often the patient continued to remain unaware of them and may well have denied that he was under stress of any sort. It is not possible to discover symbolic thinking and fantasy elaboration as a preceding or underlying feature of the physical disorder; the body seems to be on a direct short-cut circuit between the stress situation and its pathological physical manifestations. Apart from not being able to locate conscious or unconscious symbolic fantasizing, it is often difficult for the analytic observer to understand how defence, or relief from anxiety, is being obtained by the psychosomatic route, nor does it seem to offer libidinal gratification to the patient, nor help him to bear any stress and frustration; in fact, it either adds to it or displaces it. The psychosomatic patient

---

[3] A symptom can be described by the patient—e.g. a cough, or shortness of breath. The patient is unconscious of a sign—e.g. rales or other abnormal sounds in the chest, audible to the physician when auscultated with a stethoscope. Or, in the case of ulcerative colitis, the main symptom is blood in the stools, whereas a major sign is extensive change in the rectal and colonic mucosa, seen through the proctoscope or at operation.

displays either minimal, crude affect or none at all; his thinking is neither introspective nor imaginative—the Paris analysts named it *"pensée operatoire"*, which means very practical, down-to-earth; by writers in English it was simply described as "concrete thinking".

Before I proceed further, I should insert an important historical note; I said above that "from the beginning" a distinction was made between conversion hysteria and psychosomatic illness. It is, in a way, almost unbelievable, and yet it is a tribute to the intuitive and observational genius of Freud, that one of the first subjects he ever tackled was the differentiation between psychoneurosis and what he called "actual neurosis", by which he seems to have meant psychosomatic illness. As we know, Freud always hoped for a unifying physiological and biochemical theory that would explain all his psychological findings, and this very subject, still not fully elucidated by a comprehensive theory, was one of the first to occupy him. As far back as 1895, he wrote about it in the "Project for a Scientific Psychology" (1950a [1887–1902]), and he got as far as saying that the true psychoneuroses were an attempt at a symbolic solution of conflict, and that the "actual" neuroses were primarily the direct physical effects of frustration. We could still use this definition today, as a clear and simple beginning. He spotted that there was no fantasy elaboration and that the symptoms of actual neuroses were not rooted in underlying symbolism, and he based his first theory of anxiety on this finding, which stated that as a consequence of frustration—which was inevitably sexual in Freud's view—the libido was "transformed" into physiological symptoms. But he got stuck with the idea, not surprisingly, and he left it for others to work out further, which, from this promising lead, they have been trying to do ever since.

The search was extensively taken up by Franz Alexander (1950), who developed the concepts of the specificity of personality types and of bio-psychological "vectors" of a basic sort: retention–elimination, and ingestion–riddance. These still have some value; but of greater value was work in the late 1960s, which had then, when I saw my patient, only recently been completed and published by Engel and Schmale (1967). Alongside the papers on ulcerative colitis, these two workers produced extended studies of the nature of *onset conditions* in somatic responses to stress (Engel, 1962a, 1962b), and some of these still have strong predictive and descriptive value. Chief among them are (a) one that they called the "helpless/hopeless" affective states; (b) traumatic separation, particularly bereavement; and (c) the "giving-up/given-up" state. If any combination of these states of mind can be diagnosed in a patient, then the chances are that he either has, or will develop, a psychosomatic illness: that is, the states of mind seem to be truly pathogenic. To these, Alexander added vulnerability of an organ or system, which had already shown up with symptoms in childhood, and an early life situation, if it can be elicited, with certain sorts of vectors (already referred to), which may manifest as patterns in a specific sort of character and can be recognizably described—for example, early traumatic separation from the mother. Such a character may, in adult life, demonstrate features that include an apparent ignoring of stress, a physical pseudo-stamina, a strong ego ideal of independence—which in analysis is shown to conceal a passionate and infantile longing for dependence—and an insensitive, disaffected tendency to be a lone wolf.

To these phenomenological descriptions, the concept of "alexithymia", as revealed by analysis, had, in the 1960s, recently been added by Nemiah and Sifneos. It is my impression that what it referred to—namely, a kind of deficit in the ability to symbolize and fantasize, which suggested that the deficit was either inherent or produced by very early pre-speech, infant–mother disturbance—rather caught people's imagination and tended to block creative research for some years. However, it still seems to be the case that there *is* a kind of central void or inner break in mind–body linkages, which predisposes to short-cut physical reactions to stress. Alexithymia as a concept received considerable attention and research from Joyce McDougall, who had several psychosomatic patients in analysis and realized that this syndrome, from their early history, underlay the later symptoms. There is a failure of verbal communication from the mother, or primary carer, just at the time—between 9 months and 2 years—when the child is developing *thoughts and words*. The result is a sort of verbal inadequacy and the capacity to symbolize does not develop. They cannot accept or understand interpretations, and they demonstrate very literal, concrete thinking. The treatment is to try to *lend* them language, metaphor, more mobility in their mental life. McDougall's quite short book, *A Plea for a Measure of Abnormality* (1980), deals with this subject in a vividly readable way. Characteristically, what may appear to be dynamic, object-relations-type conscious fantasies existing in psychosomatic patients are usually secondary elaborations, not psychopathogenic, often acquired by an intelligent use of analytic interpretations. This feature my patient clearly showed, after several months' work, although he was also, to an extent, and always had been, capable of *conscious* fantasy.

In the 1960s, theoretically, it was inferred that bodily change evoked directly by stress had to have a biological purpose, which Engel (1962a, 1962b) approached as if the patients should show "fight-or-flight", or "conservation–withdrawal" patterns, these being associated respectively with anxiety or depression. Thus Murray Jackson (1978) described a psychosomatic response, which, insofar as life stresses reach the depths of the mind at all, was scanned by the unconscious ego, which in turn triggered an attempt at a psychobiological "adaptation". However, since it is often extremely difficult to decide how—if at all—the current physical symptoms are being positively helpful in the adaptation process, the implications for the therapist are (a) that he must try to increase the patient's capacity for speech, as I said above, and therefore for thought and insight, and then (b), thus strengthened in its coping powers, the ego should have less need for the biological arousal. Neil Miller saw this process as one of conditioning the autonomic nervous system, which is the one involved in somatization, resulting in what he called "visceral learning", until, by having learned a capacity to use fantasy, a form of emotional discharge becomes more directly available, thus reducing the often alarming physical reactions. Occasionally such patients will then show some grasp of transference and begin to understand transference interpretations.

I hope that it is possible to see by now how patchy the theory of causality and treatment still was in 1967, and, for example, how useful Winnicott's and subsequently Khan's work and also that of Bollas (on the use and abuse of an object) would have been to the analyst. Indeed, the notion of an internal projective identification, into an internal, split, bad object or part-object, which would then persecute the patient but at least discipline his violent aggression, is now very valuable in theorizing on psychosomatic states, but was then mostly unfamiliar.

Now let us turn from the background of scattered hypotheses of the time to my patient. The first thing I must admit straight away is that had I been less ignorant then and known just a little more about some of the later criteria for undertaking the psychoanalysis of these patients, I probably would have rejected him at first sight! Contraindications, even at the time, included: more than one hospitalization for severe illness of the type under review (he had had three); a dependent, impulsive, and immature personality (this was clear at our first meeting, under a light veneer of rather manic sophistication); and a negative attitude to analysis in the patient, and/or a previous failed treatment (he had had the latter, and, though only for twelve weeks, it was enough for him to come to loathe the austere and silent analyst, who conducted inpatient weekly psychotherapy as though it were the fifth year of full analysis). But the patient had subsequently seen a delightful consultant, an ex-colleague of mine, who had persuaded him to have another try, so he had some hope and some positive anticipation, at least, by the time I met him. I was keen to learn about the illness, I had a half-empty practice . . . what the hell, I took him!

During the preliminary interview, he sat opposite me in the chair; for the rest of the analysis, he lay on the couch, although such a passive description gives no real picture of him. He really *used* the couch, in a way I have only rarely seen in any patient. For one thing, he constantly turned round, often sitting up first, to check, as I eventually interpreted, that he had my undivided attention at all times. And, indeed, he had. It would have been difficult to attend to anything else with him in the room.

He was a 32-year-old Jewish doctor, a G.P. who had very much wanted to be a surgeon but had—fortunately in my view—failed the higher exams twice and given up on that. He had not been a welcome baby: he came too soon after his elder brother, and his mother had wanted a girl. His mother was said to have been depressed after his birth; she breast-fed him for a few months and then suddenly stopped. At the same time, I imagine the mother began to manifest then—if only by using the baby as a container for negative projections—a side to her that went on all through his childhood. This was an interfering inability to allow him to individuate properly and fully; it seems that he had experienced severe ambivalence from the mother and sudden loss of the breast, but at the same time, the mother—certainly as an internal object—became a close, scrutinizing, superegoish figure to him. Some of this was soon derived from the transference, which swung wildly through the whole spectrum of acute ambivalence almost from the beginning, often several times in one session. The overall effect of this was that the patient appeared to go through a series of paradoxes, so quickly would he say one thing expressing his "loving " dependence on me and then swing into a violent reaction against that fleeting feeling and upbraid me contemptuously for being useless, ungiving, and ignorant. I will give a few examples of this paradoxical mood/language selected from my notes.

In the preliminary interview he said at one point that at medical school and since he had great difficulty in socializing; he put forward the idea that people seemed shy and ill at ease with him, and he said, "I think that's something to do with my terrible temper." Yet a few moments later, after saying he did not show his temper, he controlled it completely, he added: "In fact, I don't know how to *get* angry, I never do." He added that at medical school, and since, he lived in "a nightmare of angry anxiety". Starting from that moment, I did not often take up, or point out, his paradoxes, unless I intended to go on, and make a really punchy comment from having observed one. It would have been fatally easy to get into a long-winded, pedantic speech—"Well, first you said . . . and then, soon afterwards, you said . . ." while he wriggled impatiently on the couch, soon interrupting to complain—justifiably—about my boring explanations. A brisk and pointed remark from me occurred most often either when the dual selves both appeared to be caught in the transference or—as frequently occurred later—when he was besotted with a new girl-friend and splitting everything bad about himself *and* her into me. Much later in the analysis, when I had at least attempted quite a lot of work on his marked anal qualities, he missed two sessions and spent the first one on his return talking about money. He described how he had hoarded money as a child, and how utterly anguished he would feel if I charged him *anything* for the missed sessions. (He knew I would.) A minute later he was saying fiercely: "Of *course* you should charge me, charge me double, you should absolutely *flay* me for mucking you about like that, give me a bloody good kick up the bottom as well." This threw some light on much of his apparently paradoxical talk. Projective and introjective identifications, unconscious moods, strong affects all zipped back and forth between us at such a rate that even I, short of appropriate theory though I was, realized that any idea I might have of a separated relatedness between us two individuals was inaccurate, since much of the time in his mind we were a confused unit. I should add here and now that eventually, on rare occasions, I did develop the capacity to distinguish whether this had come about *either* because he had fought his way back inside the mother *or* because his mother had projected so much of her own unbearable affect into him that his struggling identity was persecuted and overwhelmed.

To finish telling the facts of his history: in his first interview with me he said he'd been "unhappy all his life", and this, I think, was true. He described himself as wanting to get married but added that something peculiar seemed to happen with girls, he couldn't *stand* them wanting him, and as soon as he achieved what he thought was his goal—that is, getting a girl interested— he had to get away from her, and . . . er . . . he wanted to be nasty to her, he added, watching me rather warily. Oh, yes, he added almost as an afterthought, and then he had these bowel symptoms sometimes, but they weren't too much of a problem. This is absolutely typical of most of these patients' attitudes to their illnesses. This casual remark came from a doctor, who might have been expected to know something about the illness and who had been hospitalized three times, on the most recent occasion for *seven months*; yet his remark seemed completely indifferent, or detached. I wrote to the consultant at that time, a famous figure in that particular world, who described him as an extremely ill patient on admission, adding: "Initially his condition gave cause for considerable concern." He had received extensive mixed medication, two transfusions of eight pints of blood each time, and was discharged, six months before our first meeting, on a mixture of five powerful drugs, including cortisone, which in those days was given in crude, large doses. He had been seen by a consultant psychiatrist while in hospital, who said: "There is a large component of emotional stress" and advised "long-term

psychotherapy". This was when the patient then had the experience with the grim and silent analyst, which had so put him off.

The patient had vivid, almost eidetic, memories of much of his
childhood, going back to the age of about 2½. He was in some
ways more typical of an ordinary hysterical neurotic than of the
affectless, unimaginative character who appears in many case
histories. He had, and remembered, repetitive fantasies and
dreams, so, although there was a certain stereotypy about them,
he was not incapable of the activity of fantasizing itself. He nevertheless had never applied his capacity for fantasy to his illness
either consciously or, so far as I could tell, unconsciously; he was
not introspective, and he was almost always strongly resistant
and scornful the first time I would introduce an interpretation
directed at the unconscious, trying to link stresses to symptoms
in what I later realized was an object-related way. Nevertheless,
after weeks of contemptuous dismissal, he did begin to make use
of interpretations, which not only emboldened me to go on but
formed the core of a certain amount of secondary symbolic elaboration, which he began to take over as his own. He was
encouraged to build up this way of thinking by being forced to
notice that, in spite of his screams of derisive laughter and endless put-downs of me, a present symptom often yielded—and
remarkably quickly—to certain interpretations. The trouble was,
the opposite also held true. By this I mean that if, as frequently
happened, I displeased him or said something he reacted against,
he could develop a dramatic symptom within the course of a
session. For example, I would say he was showing signs of dread-
ing the coming holiday and the separation from me. "Nonsense!"
he would roar, "what a bloody-fool idea. You're so *conceited*,
that's one of the things I can't *stand* about you—oh, I must go to
the loo." And he would bound off the couch. Some minutes later,
he would return, looking pale, sweaty, shaken, but unmistakably
triumphant. "There you are!" he'd say fiercely. "I'm bleeding
again, see what you did, I haven't bled for three weeks—why can't
you keep your fucking ideas to yourself?" You will begin to see
here something of how his language was so crudely concrete and
graphic that it, in itself, spoke volumes; and also you may begin
to believe that I look back on this patient as the *noisiest* patient I
have ever treated. His body language was restless and violent—he
was always bouncing, kicking, thumping the couch, twisting his

head to glare at me; and also his speech was truly anal in its explosiveness and its vulgarity—a feature that he would often slate *me* for. One day I said something simple and, to me, obvious about shit and his penis. "Don't *use* those words", he screamed, wriggling furiously, "I can't *stand* that sort of language, I think you're absolutely *disgusting*." Thus frail, patchy, and projective were his defences against his total confused involvement in his sexuality and his gut, and his symbiotic use of me.

Yet again I have let myself be distracted from his history. The main features of his childhood and growing up were the affective unreliability and ambivalence of both his parents, his constant bullying quarrels with his little sister, his frequent, semi-willed shitting in his pants, and the fantasies he remembered. When he was six, and for some years, he played an absorbing game of cannibals, either watching them cooking a woman and then joining them in eating her *or* being the person who was stewed and eaten. Sometimes the woman, after being stripped, would be burned and then eaten by vultures. He was quite friendly with his elder brother, with whom he played endless games of rubbing bottoms and sitting on each others' faces and farting. There was quite a long period, incidentally, when he would delight in farting in sessions, which sometimes led to shitting himself slightly. I could see how I might interpret all this, but whether technically I should do anything to *stop* it, I did not know, nor would I have known *what* to say or do. He took a sadistic delight in doing anything that he thought I might not like or might find upsetting, and though that, too, could be interpreted—and was—it rarely reached a level of insight and change; the glee was too pleasurable, especially if he had regressed entirely to an anal level of behaviour in the face of sexual frustration from the current girlfriend, which happened several times in the three years.

Thus we can see that from an early age he was predisposed to using his alimentary system as his main focus or, if it were not for his alexithymia, I would say channel of communication. In the family history, he had an aunt, his mother's sister, and a first cousin, who had both died of ulcerative colitis, as he told me one day apparently without affect. But he might never have reached the point of having to be so ill if it had not been for a crucial event, which began when he was 11. His mother developed carcinoma of the breast. This would have been in 1946. She had a mastectomy and the rather crude radiotherapy that was all there then was available. It soon recurred, and by the time he was 13, she had multiple metastases, mainly in liver and bone. She lived—upstairs—for another eighteen months, increasingly ill, frail, and in pain. The original site of the operation *and* the other breast became involved in fungating secondaries, about which nothing seems to have been done, apart from regular visits from the District Nurse to dress them. Many readers will not have seen this; today it is very rare; but it was, indeed, a disgusting sight, and it smelt. My patient was in an almost unliveable, unthinkable position. He was pathologically identified with his mother anyway, he was racked with fear and guilt for all the times he had been so bad and nasty; he was beside himself with an unspeakable sadistic rage at her desertion of him through illness; and he *missed* her painfully. Already he was bereaved and mourning. Engel's (1962a, 1962b) three onset conditions all steadily mounted in him: he felt both helpless and hopeless; he was bereaved long before she actually died, and in a traumatic state of furious grief; and he felt given-up, and he gave up. He swung between ruthlessly splitting off the whole scene upstairs and a ghastly dread as the time approached each day when his father, also beside himself with helpless grief, insisted that he visit his mother for at least an hour.

The only person who in any way brought some alleviation and comfort was Mavis, who seems to have been a nurse of some sort who came to live in and was a potent force for good to the whole family. Nevertheless, the boy could not just be comforted by her presence; that would have been too simple. He longed for her love, he was jealous of her closeness to his mother, he suffered Oedipal torture over her relationship with his father, and he suspected—rightly, as it turned out—that she and his father would marry after his mother died. By this time, he projected his strong death-wishes towards his mother into his father and Mavis—in other words, he imagined they were longing for her to die. This long-drawn-out period of horror did eventually come to an end; curiously, my patient almost immediately developed a physical symptom that he had never had before, and which, after two years, he never had again. He did not even tell me about it until well into the second year of the analysis. He called it "bronchiectasis". True bronchiectasis is a chronic patch of infection in a lung that has usually undergone long-term trauma in, say, a bronchitic child. In the absence of any history, however, it seemed, in him, almost like an isolated visitation. He did not just cough, he coughed productively, as it is called, bringing up infected sputum and blood. He used this completely inexplicable weapon in a disgusting and aggressive way; he would spit this stuff on the floor and into the fire, making me think of the cannibals burning somebody. He seemed to desist at school, but at home no pleadings from Mavis or beatings from his exasperated father had the slightest effect. One can hypothesize that he was trying to eliminate bits of his internal mother's horribly damaged body. The symptom vanished when he was 17 as suddenly as it had come, but he developed diarrhoea instead—again an elimination symptom. It was significant that he told me that the first sign of the diarrhoea was bright blood, only, from the rectum, on occasions; it was months before much faecal expulsion set in. This was and is diagnostic of ulcerative colitis.

When he came to me, he had had intermittent attacks of bloody diarrhoea of increasing severity for fifteen years, culminating in the hospitalizations I have mentioned, when he always had to be transfused as a matter of urgency. Although he rather casually said he thought that sometimes they were related to external stress, he carried on with the demanding, busy life of being a medical student and then a young doctor while apparently largely denying, or split off from, the fact that he was the container of a dramatically progressive illness with a bad prognosis.

I said above that he was the noisiest patient I ever had; he was also one with whom I experienced the most packed, dense sessions. I think my lengthy note-keeping was connected with this, and also with my constantly renewed amazement that his speech was so intensely vivid—his very language "gave the game away" over and over again; and yet every inch of ground gained in insight was a battle between us. I found it difficult to believe at times that he truly *could not* hear the colourful clang associations in what he said. It was as if his secondary processes had peeled away and we were face to face with the language of primary process—I don't mean dreams or structured fantasies, as on the whole there were few of either—but the vivid concrete words and phraseology he used. A typical passage in one session was more or less as follows, and in it I think something of this stark primary-process language can be heard, full of loaded words. He was feeling small and insignificant, thinking about his father marrying Mavis, and the fact that he'd deliberately made his girl-friend wait for him last night, and then she'd been cool and uninterested in him. But, after all, he added, he didn't give a damn about her, all he wanted to do was grab her and give her a pint of the best; but she *had* made him feel humiliated, and he loathed that. I said something about his need to be in control at all times, especially of women. He said he felt much better when he thought of his new car, which was a Triumph—that was actually the name of the make—a car that was extremely popular in Britain for about fifteen years. He said he'd like to drive round now like a bat out of hell, running over things and hurting people. Having recently introduced him to the idea that there could be a strong connection between sex and aggression, I said he identi-fied with the car as if it were his powerful penis, with which he could control, hurt, and frighten people. "Don't be so *disgusting!*" he cried, "How you can say such mad things I don't know, and expect me to swallow them." Then he went right on to complain about what he called the "weedy thinness" of his own body; he was ashamed for girls to see it, especially the beautiful buxom girls he liked. "I'd never let a girl see any of me if I could help it— I wish I could just stick it in and be done and leave. But then", he added, "I can't stand a girl who gives in when I want her anyway, I *despise* her. And when they want me to wear a sheath, I could strangle them, what they don't know is it makes me feel com-pletely cut off." I reminded him he'd used exactly that phrase when his car had something wrong with it and had to go into the garage, and he missed it. "Oh, shut up, shut up", he shouted, catching my drift, "that was nothing—just a screw loose!" Then he ruminated on how he'd saved and saved for that car. "It was wonderful to feel the money piling up—I've always hoarded, you know, there's something so delicious about it. But something that was odd was that when I came to pay for the car, I just *cleared it all out*, I produced this *huge* amount of money, all ready for my lovely car, and I felt just wonderful—empty and clean, and I got my Triumph." I compared these experiences briefly to with-holding his shit till he was utterly constipated, then mother's enema would produce a huge clear-out. I added that it seemed that money and shit had something in common. "There you go!" he screamed. "You torture me with your rubbish. You've got a mind like a sewer." He bounced and kicked angrily on the couch. So I asked *him* if he could give me any ideas on other experiences that produced that lovely feeling. After a pause he remembered that his father had given him a gun when he was 10, and the feeling of shooting an animal or a bird *cleanly*—"there was nothing sexual in it", he added hastily in the middle, trying to forestall me—but the intense excitement of shooting, and then having this beautiful creature dead in his hands—there was nothing like it. "But if I just wound an animal, its screams are terrible, they go straight through me, I can't bear it, and I *can't kill it* then; I have to watch it and listen—oh, it's terrible." I thought, but did not speak, of the dying mother upstairs and the sights and sounds of her. Towards the end of her life, she had, indeed, screamed, from the pain of secondaries in the bone. Later this kind of interpretation made a lot of sense to him. In fact, for the last eighteen months of the analysis, after long concentration on the ways in which he presented, and on the transferences, he recovered a lot of feeling, from beneath his total denial of *any* feelings at all since his mother's death; the analysis moved on a long way, and he was almost entirely free of colitis symptoms.

This period, in which he discovered the enormous value to him both of tempestuous crying and of being unashamedly angry in various ways, and with me, was interrupted by one fairly brief but severe attack of the illness, which he attempted to ignore, except as a weapon against me. I was by then able to interpret a fearfully damaged bloody introject that he had to rid himself of; but also, one day I stopped listening and thinking in my customary way and just questioned him closely on the details of his current symptoms. I had become suspicious that he was operating strong denial; and sure enough, I discovered he was having between 15 and 20 bloody stools a day and felt feverish and ill. I suggested he go into hospital, and I contacted his consultant myself there and then. He was relieved and grateful. He was transfused and quickly responded to medication and, I thought, to an increased capacity to be reminded of what his body was saying. He was discharged in three weeks. That attack had been precipitated by two things: a definitive break-up with a girl he had ambivalently longed for; and a big fight with me over money.

He was not paying—that is, he was withholding my fees—and he had not paid for three months. We battled our way through that: he paid me and punished me by shitting me right out—that is, disappearing into "*proper* care" as he called it, after several sessions of dashing to my lavatory and almost forcing me to question him and take charge.

There was no doubt that in a way certain aspects of his life slowly got better. For one thing, he really worked at repairing his relationship with his father and Mavis, and so far as I know, the improvement was maintained. He managed one quite long relationship with a decent girl, though in the end he could not bear the infantile need it aroused in him, and he sadistically got rid of her. And his psychic vocabulary continued to increase, and therefore his thinking became more mobile and less stereotyped, in the teeth of all his resistances.

At the end of our third year of work, the long summer holiday loomed. He had more or less managed most of my holidays, by a mixture of intensive work beforehand, a heroic willed effort on his part to hold illness at bay, hanging on to a fragmentary good memory of me, and a certain amount of increased separation from the internal persecuting damaged object. But, paradoxically, as he made the beginnings of a truer, more whole, other-object–relationship with me, so he was more threatened by its loss. He broke down badly in that long holiday, and his consultant re-admitted him. At least he had made early contact with the consultant. He was very ill for several weeks; the possibility of a partial colectomy, with a colostomy, was discussed, as it had been before, and the final unsatisfactory reason why it was not done was that the whole of his colonic mucosa was, as his consultant wrote to me, "already shot to pieces".

The patient decided, when he recovered from that bout of illness, in what I still think was an aggressive and manic flight into health, not to come back into analysis. Although he wrote me a long and curiously appreciative and grateful letter, I found that his usual verbal give-aways also told me that he felt that I was the source of danger, and that he would be safer on his own—or rather, as he thought at that time, with his latest girl-friend. He ended his letter by saying, "It's as if I have been undergoing intensive training for a campaign, but I can't be dependent on my trainer forever, and I feel the campaign has now begun." Four months later he wrote me a very long letter, twelve pages, with the flavour of one of his packed sessions on the couch. A lot of random insights, swinging ambivalence, fragmented remarks, bits of part-objects, gobbets of news, moods, feelings. He was still with Sally, the same girl-friend, though in a more confused way. He had had another short spell in hospital, but otherwise his symptoms were what he called "not too bad". I answered his letter in general terms, but after that I never heard from him again.

Recently, I tried very hard to find him, for the sake of this paper; but he has even, significantly, disappeared from the Medical Directory, and I think that one must conclude, in view of the severity of his illness, that in all probability he is dead.

CHAPTER SEVEN

"And now for something completely different . . ."

When we consider how important supervision is thought to be during the training of a psychoanalyst or psychotherapist, it is surprising how little has been written about it. A lot of weight is ascribed to the supervisors' reports during training, and yet this job, which demands high skills, may be comparatively new ground when one has clambered up the hierarchy far enough to be asked to do it. It is almost as if it has a special sort of privacy about it, which even experienced practitioners are reluctant to open up and write about; this is so even in the case of analysts who are perfectly prepared to write clinical papers that may be very revealing of themselves at work with patients. I recently attended a meeting of training analysts of the British Society at which the subject under discussion, supervision, possibly threw a little light on this in the sense that writing about supervision may betray that we do, at times, exert "undue" influence on our students. A particular aspect—choice of super-

I would like to thank "Anne" and "Mary" for their willing help in the construction of this chapter.

visors—was discussed at length, and the problem of the extent to which the training analyst influences the choice of his/her student came up. It was suggested, discussed, and then actually proposed that the analyst should never make any sort of influential suggestion to the student but should allow absolutely free choice. This seemed to me impossibly idealistic, to a degree that is totally unrealizable. Psychoanalysts, however well-analysed and self-aware, are only human and have their share of opinions, prejudices, likes and dislikes, rivalries and favouritisms. In fact, in some ways I believe we are a rather disabled profession, disabled in the sense that some of our ideals, and perhaps neutrality and not being hampered by these human attributes, are so inordinately difficult to maintain. Too often, one can become aware that illusions and self-deception grow in the attempt to reach or maintain ideals. And the further up the hierarchy we go, the greater our authority in our own limited sphere, and the fewer the checks and balances; truly, it becomes a case of *quis custodiet ipsos custodes?*

It was partly because I became more aware of these dangers, which subtly increase with the ageing process, and partly that I was weary not only of the in-built constraints but also of the authoritarianism of being a long-term training analyst in a "reporting" Society, that I decided, about eight years ago, to withdraw from the training structure of the British Society and henceforth only take on for supervision experienced psychotherapists who were looking for a "refresher course", with whom I thought there would be a far greater chance of an egalitarian relationship. This turned out to be true, and supervision from then on became a different and delightful experience.

As it happened, my last spell of being a training supervisor was one that thoroughly confirmed my decision to withdraw; it was a perfectly dreadful experience, and I will describe it briefly, largely as a contrast to my great enjoyment with the two therapists I have chosen to present as examples of post-graduate supervision. First, I want to refer to the notion of "giftedness" in a therapist. I believe this to be a strong concept that is widely used, yet hardly ever defined; and I have never seen it written about. It is as if we all, between ourselves, recognize the phenomenon and know what we mean by it—someone intelligent, intuitive, skilful with words, warm, empathic, self-disciplined, and capable of high levels of absorption in the lives of others. Such people often have a sense of vocation to the work, freely admit that they enjoy doing it, and not infrequently describe themselves as "a round peg in a round hole". They are, it goes without saying, psychologically minded—another concept and one to which I have given attention in writing (Coltart, 1988, 1992).

* * *

Supervision of such people, even in training, is a pleasure. It is radically different from work with someone who, in some fundamental and disconcerting way, is exactly the opposite. Such a one was the last student I supervised as part of her training. How she had ever survived the interviews with the Admissions Committee baffled me. She was the only student who I ever felt should be urged to leave and change her career path, if only for the sake of her own happiness and fulfilment in life. She was not unintelligent, but she was absolutely not psychologically minded. In the way that some people are tone-deaf or completely innumerate, so she was closed to any and all workings of the human psyche. She was kind and practical, and, at least from the point of view of future patients, I did not think she would ever be actively harmful. She was completely unintrospective, and I hesitated to imagine what it was like to be her analyst; in fact, it was her analyst who had asked me to take her, for a fourth attempt at supervising. She had lost two training patients, and both supervisors had refused to undertake another. A third one had actually died— one must assume for unconnected reasons. The Training Committee had suspended her for a year but refused to ask her to go altogether: this was said to be because she had already spent nine years in analysis and five in the training, and they were increasingly reluctant *not* to qualify her, after all the time, effort, and (her) expenditure. In this way are monstrous initial errors compounded.

There was a pathos about the situation. If she had been an idle villain, it would have been easier to expel her. But she tried so hard and was still so keen. I can only say that if devotion and care are parts of the mysterious Ingredient X that helps to heal people (and I am sure they are), it was in this that my feeling lay that she would never do active harm. She would present an excruciating, detailed session of confused dialogue that was not like anything I had ever heard before—not even like conversation, which would have had its own mild value. It was a dreadful sort of psychobabble, with fairly unhappy remarks from the patient (who fortunately was not too disturbed, but who certainly did need some treatment) and almost unintelligible *non-sequitur* responses from the student. Bits of undigested theory, odd technical words, startling and confused ideas that she had hoovered up at random during the last few years were strung together in a muddled stream, which had not even the virtue of being remotely connected to what the patient had said. For example, one day the patient complained about his journey and the weather. Speedily the student intervened with what I dimly recognized as a distorted version of the Oedipus complex, which I had tried to describe to her in simple terms at our last meeting. Not surprisingly, the patient was silent for some time and then said he didn't know what she was talking about. This, in my view, made three of us. The poor student was very easily unbalanced and was never far from desperation. She slid nearer to it at this point.

I decided that I could only try to stick to the very simplest ideas of our theory and try to convey them as often as possible. I used to reconstrue the material brought, insofar as I could understand it and translate it, in such terms. I described transference over and over again and tended to leave out countertransference. She would listen to me with a fixed expression of hopeful bewilderment on her face, which tended to deepen if I referred to the unconscious, as I felt bound to do. Sometimes she would get a sudden conviction that she had not only seen, but was right about, something in the patient. Extraordinary conversations ensued between us; I hesitated to disillusion her, as her self-esteem was already low. If she *had* got hold of something, I enlarged upon it enthusiastically. Often I stressed that silence was a permissible and usually valuable quality in an analyst. I simply could not recommend qualification in my report when the time came; but neither could I commit myself strongly to an alternative. The Training Committee, with what contortions I do not know, did recommend qualification, which duly came about. The ex-student, showing a common-sense grip on reality that she had always manifested, immediately left the Society and became a G.P., in which field I imagine she was loved and trusted.

* * *

But now for something completely different, as the Monty Python catch-phrase went. I would like to describe two of the people who have come to me in recent years, when I have been available for post-graduate "refresher-course" supervision. One is very experienced, and has run a full psychotherapy practice for nearly fifteen years, as well as teaching two sessions of psychotherapy in the N.H.S. The other has been qualified, as a counsellor, for only a year but has quite a busy private practice. Counsellor trainings vary in this country; some are more "analytic" than others. Hers was about average. She had wanted to train as a psychotherapist; but she had previously been a nun, in a teaching order, for fifteen years, and money was desperately short. She took the one training for which she won a scholarship. These two women differed from each other in many ways, but they had one thing in common; it made an immeasurable difference, and was the main feature that produced such a high level of enjoyment in both their supervisions. They were both extremely gifted. With both I could thus take certain things for granted: psychological-mindedness; unceasing interest in and curiosity about the lives of others; commitment to the process; a potential for creativity.

The experienced one is Anne. With both Anne and Mary, I had long discussions about the supervision when I knew I would be writing this chapter, based on notes about their experience of it, which I had asked each of them to make. What follows is taken from those discussions and notes, with passages from their notes in quotation marks.

* * *

Anne was influenced in her work by the writings of Winnicott, on whose work she lectured widely. When I look back over her year with me, the first thing that comes to mind is the atmosphere of great good humour. We laughed for a large part of the time, although we also worked hard. I am aware that, except from certain rather esoteric philosophical angles, there is nothing intrinsically funny in our sort of work—indeed, often it is sad or anxious; but there was something in her sense of humour and mine that met, and also something in me that responded to what she was unconsciously looking for from supervision. What this was she fully realized only when we had our discussion based on her notes.

She had in her practice four frantically ill and difficult patients, all of whom she had taken on about eight to ten years ago, when her needs were different and she was simply less experienced. I am sure most analytic therapists know the state of baffled near-despair to which an exceedingly disturbed borderline patient can reduce one: Anne had wrestled alone with her four, alongside the more "normal" neurotic patients who make up a practice. The sorts of situation that can be produced, often one knows not how, are of absolute darkness, when not only does progress seem to be an impossibly distant hope, but the patient actually seems to be sliding rapidly downhill. Part of her laughter was simply relief at having someone deeply interested in them with her.

But most of our laughing was to do with our sense of being truly in a "play area", and Anne realized how much she had longed for one and how much she had missed it. This is a concept of Winnicott's (1971). A play area is a kind of "place" or state of mind into which a child, in normal development, can withdraw from the impingement of external reality and enter upon what may be a long and complex play-fantasy or game in which he can be seen to be totally absorbed. External objects, toys, etc. may be used, but as symbols of some internal reality-objects rather than as their intrinsic selves. Part of the significance of this phenomenon is that the child is not, during this time, close to, fused with, depending on the mother, though he is likely to have his "transitional object" (another Winnicottian concept for some humble object that becomes invested with "Mother" and rarely leaves the child) (Winnicott, 1971) with him. It is therefore an extremely important stage in his individuation, in which he begins to discover his self. It is not a solipsistic concept; Winnicott described the sort of treatment that works as happening at "the interface of two play-areas", and he maintained that a patient will move forward into healing if patient and therapist can thus meet. It requires confidence and skill and unselfconsciousness in the therapist and is, of course, a development of object-relations theory, and not of early classical theory, in which it would have been impossible. An experienced therapist can bring this inter-face (or its absence or failure) from the treatment into supervi-sion, where, with luck, the interface of the play areas of therapist and supervisor will then be the meeting-ground. Anne felt that because this was the setting of our meetings, she was freed from anxiety and near-despair to value herself and her way of working again. She began to re-trust her intuitions and free associations. "It liberated me into being my self again—my best self as a therapist—or perhaps I really got there for the first time." This "playing" does not happen nearly so often or so easily during a training supervision; the student is too anxious, too constrained by the requirements of the training, and has not yet approached the much more advanced state of mind in which technique can seem so natural and unselfconscious, but is based on years of hard work and is a considerable art. Anne looked back on her training as a sort of container into which she put parts of herself, which gradually learned and were retrieved, but she saw it now as very limited, both by its demands and by her own self-limita-tions, by the relatively small quantity of theory she had absorbed, and by her own narcissism. "But I've made theory my own now; before, it was something that belonged to the training, which was Out There." And I could actually see her moving about with ever greater ease and mobility in theory, and in her technique it became her servant and not her master; and she enabled me to add to this through freedom in my own ideas in our "play-area".

To link up with another concept of Winnicott's (1971), the play-area is also a "potential space". In the chapter in *Playing and Reality* entitled "Playing: A Theoretical Statement" (1971, pp. 44–62), Winnicott connects the ideas from the point of view of the therapist and sees how characteristics of the therapist's state of mind include absorption (almost a withdrawal), and this is be-cause it is dependent on inner thought and fantasy and not on external stimuli. He sees the potential space as a feature of the area that cannot easily be left, so absorbing is the creative play that happens in it; all this Anne translated in terms of her super-vision, in which she had felt absorbed, creative, and free to wander, "ploughing my own furrow". A large part of the wander-ing consisted of free association to some material earlier presented from one of her borderline patients; in this I joined, and often from this shared activity there would arise, unexpectedly, rich ideas far beyond the theme of our starting point, and enlightening to it. Anne described this experience as "validation of one's own imaginative creativity, and how to use it in technique, but all within a disciplined framework; yet at the same time the frame is now, elastic, more expandable". This was a valuable and paradoxical conjunction of ideas.

We both felt an increase in energy and alertness during and after a supervision; we agreed it had a kind of excitement about it, of a desirable sort, and we also thought that if one's reserves are depleted, one is less likely to reach this state, there is less potential for it, and one can get into a downward spiral in which further depletion of resources is likely. On the whole, though one can have inspired peak experiences while working alone with a patient, we felt that the particular energizing and high-level pleasure we enjoyed was probably a function of a particular sort of supervision, one in which an egalitarian interacting of "play" and theoretically rooted free association was the keynote alongside an absence of dogmatic "teaching", and that this was only possible when the supervisee is already very experienced (and preferably shares a sense of humour with the supervisor!).

Anne was aware that "the supervision both conveyed and confirmed the importance of faith"—by this she meant specifically faith as I have written about it elsewhere (Coltart, 1992b), which is faith in oneself, which lends itself deeply to unselfconscious attention, and faith in the therapeutic process, which it is our job to help build and sustain. Finally, as she had had no supervision since her training, she was surprised and pleased that it was "so different", and that we could share so much so openly. It is certainly true that during the training the supervisor is inevitably experienced by the student as being—and simply is—in a dominant position of authority; a lot of straight teaching of basics has to be done, and furthermore, both participants know that reports are written throughout, and that they finally weigh heavily in the assessment for qualification.

We moved about between her four most difficult patients, though sometimes we stayed with one for weeks on end; predominantly we worked on one whom I call Jane. She was an inordinately intelligent actuary in her late 20s, an example of the sort of patient whose intelligence is largely a hindrance to the therapy.

But at least she mostly managed to stay at work, even when most disturbed; she was considered to be a great asset there, if somewhat eccentric, and, indeed, she carved out for herself a niche in an exceedingly esoteric field of recondite finance, on which, during the course of her frantically difficult treatment, she became a world authority! She was what used to be called a colonial, and had come to this country impelled by a need, rather than a wish, to get away from her family. She was referred by a distinguished psychiatrist, who could not reach her at all; she was also a severe asthmatic, and she had already incorporated the asthma in a deadly acting-out. She was tall, pretty, supercilious, and mostly hostile to Anne; she never looked at her and rarely addressed her—indeed, she rarely spoke at all most of the time. The question of why did she come was probably answered by her blind love for her doctor, who thought therapy was the only hope for her eccentric and unhappy life, and also for better control of her chronically recurring asthma attacks. Anne's formulation of her, when she came to me, was that she had very little definable ego, and no boundaried self; she was almost entirely fragmented in her self, except for the professional persona, which she managed to hold together probably through intellectual fascination with an engrossing and highly ordered external object. She appeared to be totally unsuitable for insight therapy and had no interest whatever in her internal world. Nevertheless, for some years early in therapy, a passionately strong and in-love transference to Anne was detectable, which it would have been destructive to interpret since it represented a nucleus of a developmental stage where none had been before, in spite of an involved relationship, still, to her possessive and disturbed mother. Out of these transference feelings, she would bring inappropriate presents for Anne—flowers and buns and a stuffed animal—"a bizarre and noxious object", in Anne's words.

Jane would appear in sessions (always punctually) in such different personality guises that Anne was bewildered, until she finally worked out that Jane's fluid, fragile ego would present in identification with whoever she had last been with. This could be a professor, a lesbian, a male heterosexual lawyer, a butcher. Jane gave no signs of even being aware of Anne; these various people would slowly disappear, but they consistently ignored Anne. When she spoke, it was deeply impersonal. She had a rare dream in which indirectly she signalled her awareness of Anne only through projective paradox; she was "rampaging" through Anne's house, but when Anne appeared, it was only to ignore her, Jane, completely. Anne felt "a deadly exclusion", particularly at times when Jane acted out by deliberately distorting her medication or forgetting to carry it with her. She was careless and destructive with her body, which seemed like an alien object to her; her clothes were weird and ugly.

She manifested no moral sense, which I thought was a result of the very early disturbance and deprivation that we had to postulate in Jane. She never got as far as the developmental stage, probably from the age of 2 onwards, when moral sense begins to develop, primarily through guilt and concern, of both of which she seemed incapable. But she was not exactly a psychopath; it seemed, rather, that she had no sense, moral or otherwise, that actions have consequences. This was something I had encountered and written about before, in a patient brought up from the age of 3 as a Cinderella orphan in a boarding school (Coltart, 1993). For example, Jane was tenuously linked to a hospital, because of the severity of her illness. She agreed to take part in a long experimental study there, providing regular data. She fed it false information, with no sense of responsibility for truth or research, which had been fully explained and which she perfectly well understood. Another egregious example was that she had a man arrested for raping her—which he had not done, as she later said. Much of her life was lived almost by accident, or through psychotic identifications; she stopped using any medication when an uncle stopped palliative medicine, wishing to end his life from cancer. She lived in the garden, as a child, for weeks on end, occasionally fed by her sister, and unsought by her mother. She seriously planned to marry her sister.

Anne had no sense of relationship or intersubjectivity in all she was and said to Jane. Interpretations were ignored as irrelevant, yet occasionally Jane would write, or say, something that, though sounding extremely mad, also played back to Anne all that had gone before between them. Yet she did not recognize it as such and thought she might have made it up. She was often "awful to be with". I asked Anne to give me an example: she quoted Jane as saying: "I'm so sick of you and your tired optimism", in a way that was "indescribably malignant". Anne said

Jane could make her feel "morally and in every way simply *beyond the pale*". This state, after the initial flush of transference love, had gone on for years.

Anne's increased sense of freedom, aliveness, and creativeness, together with feeling less vulnerable to Jane's psychotic attacks and having a firmer foothold in the theory of psychosis, gradually, against great odds, began to affect the patient. From feeling that she did not exist, that there was no one there, even to *consider* "having relationships" with, Jane began to "become visible to the world". There was a slender increase in coherence. She had the idea, from she knew not where, that Anne was *right*, and from being violently scornful of this, she began to believe (have faith) that, since Anne seemed to continue to behave as though she and the psychotherapy could make a positive difference to her, in fact it might. The greatest gain was that Anne felt quite different, and stronger, about this extremely difficult treatment.

*   *   *

My other, completely contrasting, experience, during the same year, was with a 40-year-old woman who had recently completed a two-year training as a counsellor and was building up a private practice. She wrote me such an engaging, intelligent letter after reading my first book that I broke my intention only to accept experienced therapists, and took her on. She had been a nun for the fifteen years preceding her counselling course; her Order was a teaching one, founded by Jesuits, therefore rooted in the ideas and personality of St. Ignatius of Loyola. I had recently reviewed, for the *International Journal*, a long book on St. Ignatius by the Boston psychoanalyst (and Jesuit!) William Meissner (1992), and this added to my interest in this woman, whom I will call Mary. She too wrote a piece for me on her experience of supervision, which we discussed. It could not have been more different from my time with Anne, and yet there was this aforementioned distinct element in common—she too was very gifted, subtle and intuitive and psychologically minded; I have no doubt whatever that, had she trained with us or with one of the three or four excellent psychotherapy organizations in London, I would have supervised her in exactly the way I did under her actual circumstances now. I said to her early on: "You may call yourself a counsellor, but we are turning you into a psychotherapist. I hope you don't mind!" As a matter of fact, towards the end of her year, and in her notes, she confessed that one of the most memorable things that had done most for her was my *telling her* that I thought she was gifted. She had received an injection of confidence, affirmation, and pleasure from this that had not left her.

Yet in many ways it was a radically different experience from the year with Anne.

Mary opened her written account with a memory of often visiting her grandmother when she was small, sitting beside her on a stool, and being taught to knit. She came away cheerful and encouraged and feeling she would be good at it in time. This connects directly with *my* enjoyment of the particular pedagogic role that I had with this particular person, who was engagingly keen, hungry, and willing to learn. She said she felt "welcomed", and I recalled that to welcome her and make her feel at home and confirmed in her work was certainly part of my attitude at the beginning; it was years since I had supervised a near-beginner— in fact, I had never had someone who was so psychologically minded and open, and yet at the same time such a recent explorer in a new and entrancing field. I am very sold on the idea that a good and enjoyable life means true enjoyment of one's chosen work, and, indeed, my second book is all about that (Coltart, 1993). "Survival" means survival-with-enjoyment, not grimly hanging on. Our work can be seen as belonging to the moral order, and to do it well means an increase in genuine happiness, not only for a healing patient, but for ourselves. It is the old familiar idea of "Be good and you'll be happy"! This line of thought was, of course, familiar to Mary and welcomed by her.

To begin with, she was quite anxious and showed signs of wanting very much to please me and to appear "more proficient than I was, less of a beginner than I felt". She said three things had got her over, or through, this. One was that I had told her a little anecdote about how my analyst, on the day I qualified, said to my rather cock-a-hoop self: "Now, in ten years you'll be an analyst." I added that it was true, and it took that time for one's anxiety really to subside, and it was just the same for therapists and counsellors. The next thing was that I had taken her on "with all the gaps in my training and even though I'm only a counsellor". And the third, which I have already referred to, was that I said I thought she was talented. I do believe that in supervision, in therapy, and indeed in our ordinary lives, we sometimes need to remind ourselves that we can genuinely enhance the life of someone else if we put into a words a considered, experienced, and positive opinion of that person, rather than just thinking it. The grudging fears, often encountered in psychoanalysts, that we shall have some grim negative influence by this sort of behaviour represent one of the less attractive aspects of psychoanalysis and are, I think, rooted in a primitive, Calvinistic sort of morality, almost superstition, rather than in rational thought or even human experience.

I can probably best illustrate the character of this supervision and the many ways in which it differed enormously from the free-ranging, sophisticated, and, on many occasions, hilarious work with Anne by describing briefly one of the patients she brought for our attention and the sort of issues I found myself quite clearly "teaching her" about (an experience I had rarely, if ever, had with Anne). In the nature of things, Mary tended to get a certain number of referrals connected with the Church. One was a parish priest in his 50s. He was required to be in therapy as part of a course he was doing. Mary did not really understand him beyond a superficial recognition and knowledge of a type; this was hardly surprising, as beneath a glossy and defensive veneer he was a very disturbed man, with a severe narcissistic character disorder. She had neither the theoretical knowledge nor the technique to address this, and they both felt that they were making little headway. Mary had often nearly reached the point of saying they must stop, when "something would happen" and there was a slight sense of breakthrough, and on they went. Mary nevertheless felt frustrated and intimidated.

The priest, whom I will call Mark, had a massive defensive armour. For one thing, he carried a heavy workload, intrinsically stressful. For another, he had little sense of need, and less insight; the training requirements of his course gave him sufficient external reason to be there. Further to that, he did externalize widely, in any case. His self-satisfied and grandiose omnipotence made it almost impossible for him to see, let alone take responsibility for, flaws in his personality: if "imperfections" as he called them, were detected, he would rapidly blame his early life and his parents. This was one of the first things that Mary and I worked on—how to get him to start looking inwards, acknowledging his part in the growth of his flawed self, and that there was only stasis to be found in constant anger towards his early environment, however imperfect it had been. Of course, he was constantly alert for criticism and had a general paranoid colouring to his personality; his relationships with fellow-priests and parishioners were either rivalrous or patronizing, and only with his Bishop, to whom he felt special, did he acknowledge affection and admiration. Apart, that is, from his secret relationship with a woman in the parish, for which he had a complex system of justification.

Mark was the youngest of a large family and had grown up in an atmosphere of confusion, violence, and sexual innuendo, seeing sex as the source of unhappiness in his parents. He had an ideal vision of himself "rising above it all", especially as a celibate priest, and he frequently managed to convince himself, in his grandiosity, that he achieved this ideal, in spite of some glaring evidence to the contrary.

I used the opportunity presented by this unappealing man to develop, first, the more recent work on narcissism and its disorders and, second, to put it in the context of development theory and the sorts of neurotic/psychotic disturbances that are consequent upon difficulty or trauma in the stages of childhood. I suggested some reading to Mary—not very much, mostly the appropriate Freud papers, one or two classics (as, for example, by Abraham), and, since I had been influenced of recent years by the work of Kohut, a clear text on self-psychology (Lee & Martin, 1992). I found this sort of teaching, with such a responsive receiver, a most agreeable challenge, and it caused me to think I would look out for another novice who was committed and keen, to supervise. From Mary's notes, I extracted the points that were of most use to her in the ongoing work on Mark. She felt that she finally had a real grasp on his psychopathology, one that gave her many openings for the development of further ideas and the (very difficult) subject of technique with a narcissistic patient. Alongside narcissism, we had discussed at length the characteristics and consequences of "false self" development, which she could also now summon to the aid of her thinking. She had ceased to feel stuck and intimidated, and she found that our work on development and disturbance was applicable to all sorts of patients, with whom the treatments began to move more easily.

Rather than following the material, hoping to encounter something she could comment on, she felt capable of sustained thought and of making more focused interventions. We had done a lot of work, through Mark and other patients, on transference and countertransference—especially the latter—and she felt far more confident with them; for example, she felt that with Mark she could now translate her feelings, which were often of anger and frustration, into interpretations, rather than just sitting there stifled and seething. She got hold of the idea of the importance of having a rough treatment plan, rooted in theory; but, more importantly, she understood the apparent paradox of the value of a thought-out frame for the work, hand-in-hand with trying to observe Bion's teaching on aiming to be free from memory and desire in every session. I had stayed with this with her at some length, knowing the growing value it had had for me over the years as I came to understand it better. Again in reference to Mark, she felt there was great value in being able to listen to him more skilfully, at several levels, and therefore to formulate interpretation according to what she understood him to need, rather than being pushed about into what he wanted.

One of the subjects that Mary and I discussed at considerable length, and which I feel often does not get sufficient attention, was the place of one's own moral self in the whole practice of analytic psychotherapy. She had believed, as I am sure is common to many beginners, that analytic therapists "do not make moral judgements", and she had been alarmed and anxious when she noticed that she made them frequently, not in what she said, but in what she thought and how she reacted to patients. She thought that this was a rare problem—probably a hangover from her years in religion, her degree in theology, her whole training. She was greatly relieved when we talked this out, and I said she was not expected to give up, or not use, a huge part of her intrinsic self; I added that if any analyst or therapist ever said that we do not make any moral judgements, they were suffering from a grave delusion—the whole matter was more complicated than that, and involved self-knowledge, the practice of detachment, the unsentimental development of compassion and empathy, and the skill to translate one's countertransference into sayable language—tough maybe, but acceptable to the patient. Armed with this new awareness, Mary was able to stop unwillingly colluding with Mark's lack of guilt, his complacency and grandiosity, and to confront him with the wide gaps between his self-views, his opinions on his virtues, and the critical disdain he felt for people who actually were very like him. The treatment took a dramatic leap forward—"almost as if he had been waiting for me to help him with just this"—which I thought at one level he had.

Finally, although of course it would have been entirely inappropriate to laugh in the way Anne and I had done, I certainly did not make huge efforts to suppress my sense of humour, which has noticeably played a greater part in all my work as I have got older and freer. Along with demonstrating from time to time that humour need not be dangerous, I had also put a considerable amount of effort into enabling Mary to be tougher in her approach. It is a very common weakness in the technique of younger, or new, therapists to be far too nervous of doing wrong or upsetting the patient if they harness their aggression and use it creatively in their work. The result is often that they make no impact, convey a feeling of lack of confidence, and tend towards the sentimental, as a kind of reaction formation to their anxiety about being tough and clear. I was delighted when I read in her notes:

> It could all be too rich an experience, too heady a wine, but humour and a kind of robust irreverence give it a very human feel. That's been important for me. I have a tendency to feel I have to be like God, over-responsible for my clients' well-being, able to make all things well, more aware of fragility and the danger of doing harm than of the resources of the person and their other supports. . . . I am not the saviour of the world!

* * *

I hope I have managed to convey the many pleasurable rewards of a decision late in life to cease to be an authority, abandon the demanding field of training, and hand-pick a few really interesting post-graduate psychotherapists whose gifts and personalities appeal to me, and then set out with them on a new journey of discovery.

CHAPTER EIGHT

Buddhism and psychoanalysis revisited

T he Buddha did not reach his Enlightenment until he was 40, and, contrary to what some people seem to believe about him, he was not then swept off into the heavens and did not just disappear in a radiant cloud. He continued to live the life of a wandering mendicant, but his main aim was to convey the essence of what he now knew to any who wanted to come and learn from him. He gathered round him a group of people whom he ordained as the first monastic order, and it was they primarily who received his teaching, though anyone could come and listen; and it was they, or people whom they in turn had taught, who wrote down soon after his death a lot of what he had said. Nevertheless, there is also a long unbroken oral tradition said to stretch from the Buddha himself through many generations of the Theravada monastic order, branches of which we have in Britain today. This now covers a period of almost exactly 2,000 years. The Buddha had a memorable style, he told a lot of stories that show us what an astute psychologist he was, and he also had a knack of grouping things so that they hung together; one could rapidly learn the essentials of what he taught, and then take them away and start trying to absorb them. Thus he taught what have come to be known as the Three Signs of Being, the Four Noble Truths, the Five Hindrances, the Six Attributes of Personality, the Eightfold Noble Path, and the Twelve Steps of the Wheel of Life. If you memorize these, you've really got Buddhism at your finger-tips, all you have to do is live it! For our purposes, I shall outline the Three Signs of Being and the Four Noble Truths, and I shall touch on the hindrances, because through all these, keeping one's mind flexibly open, one can draw continuous close parallels with what psychoanalysis is about.

The Three Signs of Being are inescapable, universal, there's nowhere you can turn where they will not be found to be true; our interest is primarily in how they manifest in people. They are: *Suffering, Impermanence* or *Transience,* and *No-Self. Suffering,* as used by the Buddha, is a wide-ranging, comprehensive term. We tend to think of it only in connection with illness or grief, and since some people are spared these, we have to look elsewhere for the Buddhist claim that it is universal. For one thing, its meaning expands—we think first of pain, physical suffering, or fairly acute emotional dis-ease. But the Buddha defined it more as covering all the fractional shades of feeling on the negative side of contentment or equanimity; for example, since much of our lives is made up of wants or needs, some instinctual and vital, some fanciful or luxurious, we frequently encounter frustration in many forms. Although not usually serious, the Buddha includes this in *Suffering.* A variation of that, which one would not normally think of, is the let-down, or feeling of being balked or deprived, when something pleasant, which one is enjoying, stops or goes away or changes for the worse. A little imagination tells us that any such sufferings, if magnified and put into context, can become symptoms, and as such may well be brought for therapy. Some of the sufferings that get that far are, in the West, rather recherché; I don't suppose the Buddha saw many people with anorexia nervosa, for instance. An affluent society brings its own suffering in its train—and not only an affluent society, but a morally shallow culture: our culture, in the post–World-War-Two years, has become one in which the inculcation of morality, or any form of self-discipline, are subjects rather for derision or neglect than for striving; instant and then sustained gratification is not only sought after and expected, but demanded as a right. Inevitably this brings massive disappointment and frustration behind it, which people have come to regard as suffering, and what is more, suffering not of their own making; this would involve the effortful assumption of responsibility, which seems deeply unappealing and the opposite of gratifying. I would be interested to know how many of you agree with this point of view; sometimes I ask myself whether it is not egregious or tiresome, and simply the result of me becoming old and world-weary. But it does pay to examine the notion of suffering through this wide-angle lens; one soon begins to get the hang of the idea that it is a universal manifestation.

The second Sign of Being is usually translated as *Imperma-nence* or *Transience*. Things don't last. This is a fairly easy one to accept, I believe, so long as we remember that the Buddha was making *no exceptions*. By the way, it is valuable, when contemplating the Three Signs of Being, to keep them somewhere within the same bracket. The Buddha often stressed, in the way he taught, how much most of what he was saying is interrelated. It is a satisfying logical experience to notice this as one works through the basic teachings, tabulated in the rather formal, often numerical way I referred to above. Transience, for example, often causes suffering.

The third Sign of Being is at first a harder one for Westerners to accept, or understand. It is the doctrine of *No-Self*: this is called *Anatta* in the original Pali, which itself is rooted in Sanskrit. The word for a person, or being, is *Atta,* or *Atman.* Hindu teaching holds that we go through many lives, gradually purifying ourselves, until, when perfection is reached, we are absorbed into the Universal *Atman,* which translates fairly easily as God. The Buddha, however, had seen that there is no-self, *An-Atta,* and no supraordinate, transcendent *Atta* or *Atman.* This was one of the main ways that the development of Buddhist thought in India diverged from Hindu. And, as I said just now, it is the strangest to Western minds because we are so steeped in the Judaeo–Christian culture, which is monotheistic, and in which human beings have souls that are not only in the care of the one God, but are also eternal. Mohammedan teaching does not differ at this level, and thus we see that of the great religions of the world, Buddhism is unique in saying we have no abiding self, or soul, and that there is no God, not under any designation. Since about the mid-nineteenth century, there have been some attempts by serious, well-intentioned people from a Christian background to create a blend of Christianity and Buddhism, and some religious communities have been set up based on these hybrid lines. One or two have had some apparent success during the lifetime of their enthusiastic and even inspiring founders, but they do not last, and I believe this to be due to a failure to take seriously the absolutely fundamental incompatibility that lies beneath many more superficial philosophical and moral concordances. I do not intend to spend any time or effort trying to convince you of the truth of *Anatta* but will only say that if one sticks to the principle of looking at the teachings from an interrelated viewpoint, then it may become a little easier; for one thing, the notion that there is no self or soul causes many people real pain, or suffering, and even when insight is developed, there is often a bitter struggle between two opposing thought trains; but, secondly, it is *Transience*, the second Sign of Being, that offers a real bridge. If we accept that the Buddha was completely serious when he said that *everything* is impermanent, then this must include the human spirit or soul or, as I prefer to say, the *idea* of the human soul. I will return to this from a particular standpoint later.

It is my contention that the practice of psychoanalysis in harness with the practice of Buddhism is not only harmonious, but mutually enlightening and potentiating. There does not seem to me to be any area of absolutely radical disagreement or clash between the two, in the way there is at the deeply theological level between Christianity and Buddhism. The first two Signs of Being are manifest day-in, day-out in analysis; people come to us because they suffer—that is almost axiomatic. And we can be helped in one of our own attitudes as therapists if we deeply believe, because in our bones we *know*, that everything is impermanent; nothing lasts, not even the most painful suffering. Of course sometimes it changes for the worse—it is not necessarily a doctrine of mindless optimism. And we certainly would never either say, or even think, "Oh, well, it won't last" as a sort of dismissive pseudo-comfort. This would be just ignorant and unkind, in that we would not be taking a sufferer seriously in the here and now. But I am also trying to point up the value of some of the teaching to our own personal underpinning philosophy of life, and there it can be a valuable adjunct.

There is, of course, or appears to be, a knottier problem when it comes to the third Sign of Being, because all our theory and practice of therapy seems to hinge on working with the self of another person, and trying to repair that on-going self in an effort to relieve the suffering. I shall come back to this, but first I want to turn to the Four Noble Truths as taught by the Buddha, because they contain the essence of our working theory in a nutshell.

Try to bear in mind a rough idea of what you think psychoanalysis is, and what, as a therapy, it is for, as I spell out the Four Noble Truths. The first is that suffering exists; wherever you turn, you will encounter suffering, particularly if you remember the expanded definition I gave earlier. We do not have to look very far in our profession; people consciously bring their suffering to us, though they may be unconscious of what much of it is about, and that is one of the things they need us for. The Second Noble Truth is that suffering arises, that is to say, has causes; this Truth links fundamentally to what is called the Great Wheel of Life, or what the Buddha taught as the Law of Dependent Origination. This Law is worked out in twelve stages, whereby being born is, or appears to be, the so-called first step, and then life works through to death by the various stages, so that the logic of the great wheel is seen in how the chain of causality operates throughout life, how one thing leads to another. We do not need to bother about the fact that a wheel is circular, which is achieved by the fact that in Buddhist theology death leads on to birth and life again. This part of the doctrine is not only referring to death—of the body—as the major and only truly predictable event of life; it is refined so that it refers to the innumerable small deaths and births of which life is made up all the time, and it is far more useful and interesting to us to regard it from this angle. For example, you are not, at this moment, quite exactly the same person as you were when you got up this morning. It is a way of reflecting on the constant flux and process of living that we are engaged upon. Where the circle, and the Second Noble Truth, are important to us as therapists is in the contemplation of detailed chains of causality, so that in self-reflection on our being-in-the-world we learn to see how we ourselves set up far more of our own conditioning than we probably consciously realize, and thus how we originate our own suffering. This is something we constantly aim at understanding in analytic therapy, largely in order to reach the stage of the Third Noble Truth.

The third is that suffering has an end. There are ways, some more skilful than others, of bringing about the cessation of suffering; some of these ways are part of our daily technique. "Skilful", incidentally, is a favourite Buddhist word. The Buddha often referred to what he called "skilful means" of understanding suffering so that it could be helped to change for the better; one of the words for "skilful" in Pali is also translated as "wholesome", which is a nice, old-fashioned word that makes one think of health.

Then we come to the Fourth Noble Truth, which is where the Buddha really managed to condense all his moral teaching into one compact idea; that is, that suffering can be alleviated by coming to know, and then trying to stick with, the Eightfold Noble Path, or what is also often called the Middle Way. Whenever the Buddha preached on the Four Noble Truths, he always enumerated the individual steps of the Eightfold Noble Path, indicating how important they are. He would also dwell on each step separately, or consider them in little groups of two threes and a two. You need to make allowances for the traditional way the steps are set out, which sounds a bit extreme and pious, but if you follow the spirit rather than getting hung up on the exact letter or criticizing how they are translated, I think you will see, contained in the path, not only the moral teaching of Buddhism, but also, insofar as we are aiming at many of the same goals in analytic therapy, that psychoanalysis, too, cannot help but be a moral system, whether we think of it like that or not—indeed, whether we like it or not. The eight steps are as follows: right understanding, right thought, right speech, right action, right livelihood, right effort, right mindfulness, right concentration.

These steps are not to be thought of as in an unchanging order, or to be followed like real steps, one after the other. Again we are in the presence of a series of interrelated ideas, each of which bears on all the others. Since thought and speech tend to be linear, they have to be set out as though they were in sequence, but this is misleading. What is emphasized is the practicality of Buddhist morality, and the fact is that the Path has nothing to do with worship or prayer in the sense that those of us from a Christian culture would understand the terms—in fact, it is not apparently "religious" in any usual sense at all. This might appeal to psychoanalysts, many of whom might well acknowledge that ethics inevitably has a part to play in our profession, but who shy away in something very like terror if religion is so much as mentioned. The fact that some of them display an extraordinarily religious devotion, even fanaticism, to some of their doctrines, and even to some of their leading figures, is a fascinating subject but not one to waylay us here.

Neville Symington has been one of the first, at various points in his writings, to confront the fact that in doing psychoanalysis we are engaged in a moral pursuit. Freud was so busy dismissing all religious practice as neurotic and assuring us that he wasn't particularly concerned with people, only with the scientific study of the human mind, that he failed to notice that one of his central, if unacknowledged, aims was to relieve suffering and thus make people "better". A fairly brief reflection on the ambiguities of the concept of "getting better" opens us without difficulty to the possibility that there is a hidden but powerful moral element in our profession. While it is interesting to note that many analysts seem to be nervous about acknowledging this, I do not think I need to labour the point in continuing to observe parallels between what we do and what the Buddhist teaching is about.

Linked to a reluctance to take responsibility for the moral structure of psychoanalysis is another quite powerful myth, which is that we do not "educate". Certainly we do not set out the theoretical aspects of our free associations to our patients' material in a didactic way or instruct them to learn their lessons. For one thing, as Freud said in his paper "Wild Psycho-Analysis" (1910k), that would be like handing round menu cards in a time of famine. But if we really believe that the whole process of working-through during the involved processes of an analysis is not to do with slowly educating the emotions, then we are deluded. A piece of emotional insight, which may arise during an analytic dialogue, provides not only a motivation for change, but the beginnings of clearing a way forward where previously an impassable tangle had kept us perseverating in a repetition compulsion of an old conflict. The process itself, to which the analyst contributes his thoughts and interpretations, is, in the best sense, educative. The ego expands, changes, takes in something new.

The technique in the Buddhist practice is different, but there may well be final common pathways. In Buddhism, there is no particular emphasis on dialogue; rather, the practitioner listens as attentively as possible to a teaching, or hears some of the sayings of the Buddha read out, or takes part in a chanting, but the absolutely fundamental daily practice throughout Buddhist culture is meditation. The last three sections of the Middle Way refer to this: right effort, right mindfulness, right concentration. Mindfulness is a central concept in Buddhism and refers to the desirability of using attention throughout waking life; and right concentration refers to the special, so-called "bare attention" during meditation. It is as well to have been taught one or two good basic meditation techniques by an experienced meditator early on in one's Buddhist life, because from then on it is so central, and much of the healing of the mind from suffering comes about as the result of meditation. During meditation, there is a lowering of the threshold of consciousness, and in the steady inward looking that accompanies conscious focusing on the breath, the energy withdrawn from our usual centre of consciousness, the ego or I, activates the contents of the unconscious, and the way is prepared for *samadhi* or deep concentration. In *samadhi*, or at least its early stages, we do not exactly *think*, but rather observe certain psychological phenomena. For example, being unhampered temporarily by conscious assumptions, we can see the Law of Dependent Origination, and the second and third Noble Truths, with clarity—we see how a certain emotion has a chain of causality and has an object or objects; it can be stopped, re-routed, or transformed by the simple fact of steady bare attention. This slowing-down of a process, which can lead to ego-transformation, is one of the great advantages of the clarity of mind already prepared for by the earlier stages of the meditation. For example, we may receive a sense impression, which produces various feelings, but if we can pause there and register them with bare attention, we are not necessarily led on into a desire to do something else—say, meet what we fancy to be a need, which could often lead to further feelings, or some physical activity, or tears. As a great teacher, Nyanaponika Thera, says in *The Heart of Buddhist Meditation* (1962):

> The curt and simple, but repeated registering of the nature of feelings just arisen will have greater influence on the emotional life than an emotional or rational counter-pressure by way of eulogy, deprecation, condemnation or persuasion.

I must stress here that transformation frequently occurs, if slowly, as a result of this observation, *not* of thinking, during the meditation itself. Of course, the phenomena arising can be thought about and worked on further after the meditation is over, but it is important to clarify here that, though it may not be obvious to us how it works, ego change for the better is perfectly possible and frequently comes about. There is apparently a powerful creative element in non-discursive discernment, and I am inclined to think this functions in analytic insight-achieving more than we realize. When we have seen something steadily and seen it whole, it tends to lose its tenacious aura or importance in our personal structure and seems simply to begin to diminish; either that or, as we lessen our possibly pathological attachment to it, we seem to move psychically further away from it, and its hitherto powerful, apparently fixated place in our psyche shrinks. The intellect itself is possessive, and merely thinking about something can harden it up and confirm its importance to our conscious self, as well as leading us to make irrelevant judgements, such as believing that we need it, or that our attachment to a certain pattern is indissoluble. However hard we may "work at" being in analysis, I think it is this intellectual component that can get in the way. The conscious intellect may have knowledge, but it is the great sea of the unconscious that is the source of wisdom; I believe this accounts for the frequent occurrence of insight, and realization about one's own analysis, which can take place in retrospect.

The word "realization" brings me back to the third Sign of Being, or *Anatta*, or *No-Self*. The link is that "self-realization" is an important term in Jungian psychology, where the process is synonymous with "individuation". Jung would also allow that the concept of awakening can be the same as self-realization, itself a dynamic effect of either analysis, or some religious practices that are not all arbitrarily controlled by voluntary acts of will. One of the translations of Buddha is The Awakened One, and awakening has been described as "coming into the Buddha-mind". Buddhism itself, a pragmatic religion, conveys that awakening is a process that continues throughout life—life as led in the religious context, that is, and not a sudden event bounded entirely by Enlightenment. Certainly the Buddha is said to have reached his Enlightenment at a particular point in time, after seven days and seven nights in continuous *samadhi* under the bodhi-tree, but this is the sort of definitive Event that tends to happen in the lives of great religious leaders and is no doubt fed, if not entirely created, by myth and legend. If the Buddha were to use the language of today, I think he would say that, for someone trying to lead the religious life, including lay people, awakening is continuous or happens in small increments and aims at overcoming the suffering of human conditioning by a process of ego-transformation; what he would *not* say is that the aim is ego-destruction or self-negation. Buddhism is widely misinterpreted in the West as being nihilistic, one implication being that the third Sign of Being is somehow struggled for with gritted teeth, as if the self can or must be destroyed by force. This view, which suggests an exhausted human body containing an ugly, boring void and worse off than one was before, is not at all what *Anatta* means. *Anatta* is not something that we *create* as a result of strenuous practice; it is a state of being that *is so*, which we may come to realize, or we may not.

In truth there is a delightful paradox in the teaching, and I think it relates much more closely to what we can understand of Winnicott's theory of True and False Self than to any notion before which our conditioned Western minds largely recoil—that of a kind of nothingness in the midst of life. I must say, this in turn makes me think of nothing so vividly as Piglet looking into the pit in the wood and seeing Pooh with his honey-pot stuck on his head. Piglet ran from this dreadful vision screaming: "Help, help! A horrible heffalump! Holl, holl, a herrible hoffalump!" and later described his vision as "a sort of Nothing!" The Buddha knew perfectly well that people need living, intelligible imagery, compatible with their subjective experience, and that language provides it; we live in a contingent world of people and objects where only the concept of self, operating interactively with other selves, makes any kind of sense. The language in which the Buddha teaches is full of acute psychological observations, of descriptions of people deploying their egos in relation to a contingent conditioning world of people and events. He would perfectly well have understood a therapy directed towards slowly dismantling a constricting False Self and encouraging the awakening and growth of the True Self. He was well aware, in fact, in the language of the time, that in order to attain deep *samadhi*, abandoning one's sure anchorages in the conscious self and opening oneself to the strange elements of the deeper unconscious, paradoxically a strong and fairly stable ego is necessary, else an unwanted psychic disintegration can begin to happen. This, in fact, is what is known to occur in some unfortunate cases where meditation has been poorly taught by an inexperienced amateur to someone whose mental health is by no means sound in the first instance, but who is led by enthusiasm or sentiment into a territory he had better been strictly warned off. This kind of breakdown, of which I have seen at least three cases, should provide a strong warning against treating meditation as if it were some sort of alternative health gimmick; there has grown up an unfortunate tendency towards this in the West, and I have encountered people who have embarked on it in this spirit and then become speedily disappointed when they sit two or three times, doing I know not what, and then say fretfully that "nothing has happened". Quite what they anticipated is difficult to elucidate, but at least a mild disappointment is better than the disintegrating confusion and loss of grip on reality that can occur when this powerful instrument is casually handed on, by an unprincipled, inexperienced teacher, to an ignorant recipient searching for an undemanding remedy for dissatisfaction with his life.

We need to see that there is a widespread acceptance of convention in the Buddha's teaching; the conventional way of thinking about ourselves in the world, living a life, with as much normality or as much psychopathology as it is one's destiny to encounter, uses the concept of an on-going self without difficulty because within the limits of language, thought, and imagery we *seem* to ourselves to be regular identities, whom we can remember stretching back through time and whom we daily recognize as having characteristics and features that do not change much from day to day. This, of course, is how we get to know ourselves and other people. The third Sign of Being to which the Buddha refers operates on another philosophical level altogether.

What can be of more immediate interest to us here is seeing how closely Buddhism and psychoanalysis are a study of the Hindrances; these are the aspects of personality that make it difficult to achieve happiness, equanimity, and morality. They are: rage or hatred, greed, anxiety, laziness, doubt, and, as a background spin-off or accompaniment to all of them, delusion.

We would probably use illusion as the more regular translation of this one. I do not think it is difficult to recognize in these the constituents of most of the symptoms we encounter in the consulting-room. We could probably all rapidly work out how the various hindrances express themselves in terms of symptomatology, but I think probably the most interesting is illusion; it says something of how psychologically sophisticated the Buddha's views were and how acute and subtle his observations of human nature, in its struggles to move towards awakening or becoming the true self. You could say that the whole practice and training in Buddhism is dedicated to the attainment of the awakening of the real or true self by a process of breaking through the illusions of the human mind. There was an interesting psychoanalyst called Karen Horney, who was in some ways a devoted follower of Freud and in others a stern critic. Her theory of neurosis gives a central place to the importance of illusion. It was not that Freud did not recognize illusion—indeed, he even used the word in his late book on religion, *The Future of an Illusion* (1927c). But Horney placed it at the centre of her theory of neurosis. She stated that the core of neurosis is the early establishment of an ideal self-image, which becomes identified with the idealized self, as a defence against anxiety and insecurity, and that this self represents in the individual a dominating, controlling illusion; illusoriness therefore permeates all characteristics of the false self which the person tries to live out as his being-in-the-world, since he comes to believe that this person, created by anxiety and fantasy, is not just an ideal to be lived up to, but is actually him. There are ways in which I see Horney's work as a forerunner to that of Kohut, since it focuses on a failure to progress beyond an exaggerated and distorted narcissistic stage of development; but in spite of her loyalty to Freud and her recognizably classical style of working, her independence of thought put her outside the mainstream of psychoanalysis, and I have not come across any acknowledgement of her work in Kohut's writings.

I will give an example. Let us say that the natural tendencies of the individual are towards compliance and dependence; he may create through his imagination a persona of pacificism, goodness, saintliness, patience and a devotional sort of life. (It is hardly fair to call this creature "he", as I am sure we will all recognize certain females of our present or past acquaintance, especially if we have ever moved in Church circles.) Even lay people who are not particularly psychologically minded will sense the unmistakably phony quality of this inauthentic self that is built around and upon an illusion. The illusion is, of course, grandiose, because idealized, and there are distinct claims that it makes on other people; other people should fulfil her demands, in order to reinforce the security of her false self; her demands, which Horney calls "neurotic claims", are self-righteous and egocentric, though often in the guise of being charitable; they disregard the needs of others, or the necessity for effort and endurance—naturally, since they are half-consciously intended to be a short-cut onto the Middle Way, not a true striving. The type we are considering claims total acceptance, affection, and care, and devoted admiration for her superior spiritual achievements as manifest in her saintly character; help at any time, frequently solicited, is to be unstintingly given, and the helper should regard it as a privilege, not a chore. If, however, her claim meets with frustration, or any such form of suffering is imposed, an uglier side appears, indignation, hostility, and accusations of unfairness and neglect, which she will abundantly justify in terms of her own deserts and the other person's meanness. Depression, irritability, and self-pity may follow, and the frustrating person is freely criticized. This situation occurs fairly often, as she has, of course, little or no capacity for friendship, and the commonest reaction of others to her is one of rather uneasy and mistrustful dislike. This in no way coincides with her own conception of their view, which is assumed to be one of caring and humble admiration. Nevertheless, since she is not completely dislocated from reality, she is also suspicious and somewhat paranoid, which feeds her criticism of them. However, there *are* also demands made on the self, and she feels that she should always try to be—or, more importantly, be *seen* to be—loving, understanding, self-sacrificing, and sensitive to others. Since all these requirements are the product of illusion, they are doomed to frustration, as they are rooted in her narcissistic fantasy and there is no muscular moral apparatus to render them authentic; this produces depression, strain, guilt, and a form of self-hatred, often projected. Naturally, spontaneous feel-

ings and self-expression, thoughts, and beliefs are in short supply, and there is a deadly artificiality about the character.[1]

She will come to analysis unaware of the malignant illusion at
the core of her being, but complaining of depression and inertia,
probably paranoid in colouring; often there are some sorts of
psychosomatic manifestation, since she cannot truly verbalize
her condition. Therapy is a long tough haul, as the immensely
complex false self has to be gradually dismantled. The therapist
will meet with resistance and negative transference all along the
line, the latter rooted in the original relationships that were unsatisfactory enough to have impelled the creation of this false self,
whose self-esteem lies only in her own delusional estimation of
how loveable, good, and compassionate she is. These attributes
have defended her from recognizing her anxiety, shallowness,
and helplessness, but since they are illusory, they are also basic-
ally fragile. She may be forced to feel shame and humiliation as
the process of therapy gradually reveals the meretricious and
threadbare quality of the source not only of all her pride but of
her very being—that is, her saintly character. The false self is not
given up without a struggle or without many twists and turns,
such as rage, retaliation, appeasement, flattery, panic, more
physical symptoms, and so on. The whole therapy has to concentrate on being a well-judged, sensitive, disillusioning process, as
Horney calls it. But since so much psychic energy has gone into
the creation, much can be freed, and the ultimate prognosis is
good, provided the patient can trust the fundamental good will of
the therapist. Ultimately, the true self will grow apace. With any
luck, she will develop a sense of humour and irony with which to
look upon the wreckage of her previous self. There is also something amusing to a Buddhist therapist in the realization that it is
only *then* that a person may come to realize that the achieved self
is, after all, an illusion—is, in other words, a no-self! But since it
is not technically or ethically a part of any analytic therapy to
introduce the subject of religion if it is not raised by the patient
(and even if it is, teaching or conversion is contraindicated), it is
unlikely that she will be required to contemplate this idea.

---

[1] When I first gave this paper, a young man in the audience later
asked: "How come you know my mother so well?"

The paradox that is perfectly viable is that the Buddha taught the sorts of practice, including moral discipline, that can strengthen a healthy or a healing Real Self, awakening out of neurotic False Selves, yet at one and the same time would be teaching that there *is* no True Self in the sense of an unchanging identity. It is the notion of a central solid soul that the Buddha was trying to combat—a soul that is always recognizable to the self and to God and not only persists through this life, but moves over, unchanged, retaining identity, either into eternity, with God (the Judaic and Christian view), or into the next incarnation. The Buddha remained studiedly non-committal on the question of reincarnation, but many Buddhists believe in it, and he might well allow that the very stuff of "life" itself is not extinguished and may animate another being, and another, and another. . . . What he taught against is the narcissistic delusion, dear to the hearts of humans, that I, me, in this identity that I know (or think I know) so well, will go on and on and on through thousands of years. The second Sign of Being rescues us from this, or should, even if the third seems too hard to grasp. If all things, all phenomena, all beings are transient, then there is no abiding me to go on all these endless journeys. Of course, in psychoanalysis we behave *as if* there is a self that recognizably continues, suffers, hopes for treatment and happiness, struggles for changes, knows itself often quite deeply, and experiences degrees of self-realization. But then so do we in Buddhism. It is what gives depth and meaning to life.

After all, we can't just ruminate endlessly on the problem contained in this verse:

A Buddhist once said: "To deny
That this I is an I is a lie;
For if it is not,
I should like to know what
Is the thing that says: "I am not I."

CHAPTER NINE

Endings

I t would be really interesting to take people's first associations to my title. By now you are accustomed to it, you have known for a while what this talk is called. But supposing I had just now announced it. There are lots of possibilities; because this is a psychotherapy audience, some of you might think immediately, almost as an assumption, that it refers to the end of therapy or analysis. You will not be disappointed, but to confine ourselves to that would be to limit our field.

My own very first association was an image. The image had no people in it, it was of wintry fields, not snow-covered or sunlit, but greyish and rather wet. It was accompanied by a very faint bodily sensation, of slight chill, and this was followed rapidly by an emotion that was distinctly bleak and, I suppose, lonely. All this happens very fast, of course, and is even difficult to break down into elements—but we have to learn this skill, that of constant detailed scanning, when we do our sort of work, so it should not be strange or new. So far, there were no words. Things

---

This paper was first given as an Arbours Public Lecture on 17 November 1993 in London.

speeded up; the greyish fields flooded and froze over, some people were skating, and the ice cracked. The water was not deep, so I can deduce that at this point it was not a particularly aggressive fantasy. It was, still, more bleak and desolate than dangerous, but at least there were now some people. At about this point, a kind of self-consciousness intruded, and with it came more thoughts. I did think about endings of treatments, but the first and stronger thought was about death.

So I reached the point at which Ending is one of the greatest of all human concerns, the only one that none can escape. I was not aware that I myself thought about death as particularly bleak or desolate, though I know there are those who do. Sometimes I think, like Peter Pan, that it could be a big adventure. Mostly, I think it will be extremely *interesting*, and it seems to me as if almost the greatest blessing that life can grant is to go consciously into one's own death. It is maddening not to be able to write a paper about it afterwards; but to greet one's death, to observe and inspect it, would feel like a fitting ending—particularly to a psychotherapist's life.

I said just now that death is the greatest of all human concerns, and the word "concern" feels appropriate here. I am not, of course, using it as it is so often misused today, when it means worry. It is a far greater word than that. It is not delusional or shallow, as a worry can be. Worries can be real and frightening, but more often they are transient, invented, silly, or imaginary. When they get serious, they are more properly called anxiety. Some people seem not to feel comfortable, or even as if they are behaving in a moral way, unless they are worried about something or someone, or even several things at once. Such people are rather tiresome and are not life-enhancers, since they can often convey the restless sense of worry to others or, worse, become boring by grinding fruitlessly on about it, unable to receive comfort or reassurance. I do believe the habit of worrying fades as people grow wiser and older and especially if one does some constructive work on it. One of the best bits of teaching I ever heard when I was a medical student was from a consultant, on the difference between worry and concern. "Try not to *worry* about patients", he said, "and certainly don't ever take worry home with you overnight. Be concerned for the patients, always— you will find that with true concern, you can leave them behind when you aren't with them. Work out the difference." This repays reflection, especially in our profession. I think it is natural for a student or a fairly newly qualified therapist to be anxious a lot of the time about the work; anxiety is, or can be, a state on its own, somewhere between worry and concern. But the first ten years or so in practice are the time for working through anxieties and learning the radical difference between worry and concern.

In life itself, apart from the strange lives lived out in the consulting-room, a lot of people are worried about death—at least, they are often not sure if it is death or dying they are worried about. I think it is more likely to be dying. At any rate, they are worried and could be said to be in a chronic state of anxiety about it—their own death, that is. Such people often give little conscious thought to the deaths of others: there is though another group of people, usually those who have experienced severe traumatic loss in their lives, who are deeply anxious some of the time about the death of a loved person and fear little for themselves. From being within relatively normal limits, both these sorts of worry about Ending can grow to monstrous proportions.

I once analysed a man whose anxiety about his own death was pathologically severe. He was only ever free of it for a few hours, then it came creeping or crashing back. He would wake up in the night and lie there in a panic about the fact that he was going to die. He had brought this monosymptomatic anxiety to analysis several years before, and, as luck would have it, first one, and then a second, analyst had died on him—not literally during a session, but in the middle of an active working treatment. It was almost as if a malignant Fate had got it in for him, and naturally he had a paranoid feeling about that. However, although he often bewailed his misfortune in losing two apparently healthy though ageing analysts, one had to steer back past them as, strictly speaking, they were irrelevant to his psychopathology. I was rather flattered, ignorant young ass that I was, to be asked by a little group of senior analysts to take him on, soon after I qualified. Looking back, I think everyone had become magically superstitious, and they were saving their own faces by being flattering to me. Of course, it was my youth and vigour they were after, not my precocious talent.

He was in every way a most unsuitable patient for psychoanalysis, and I say this well aware that at least three analysts took him into five-times-a-week treatment. It just goes to show *something*, which I will not deal with here, about the mixed reasons why people get into analysis. He was not suitable, and today I hope I would not even consider him. He was exceedingly difficult to work with: he was a cold, cruel, sentimental, and deeply narcissistic man, and for quite a long time I was of the opinion that his fear of death was a crippling fear of his superego, which would finally punish him for his emotional and character defects. In fact, I still think this may have been so, although the narcissistic horror was deeper than that; but he was completely non-responsive to interpretations of any sort. He was not even compliant or courteous about them, the way many frightened people are. Things had gone too far for that. He did not at all like me, and he tended to despise women generally. Occasionally, he would consider something I said for a short while, then dismiss it and plunge back into his solipsistic ruminations.

It took me about eighteen months to come to the supremely simple formulation, which eventually I interpreted, that in his view—and intention—we were locked in a fight to the death. This connected with his early history, as well as with the deaths of his previous analysts. He did listen to this, and his ultimate re-action to it, about a year later, was to leave. Contrary to what my colleagues had thought, my comparative youth and health was not a mark in my favour at all so far as the patient was con-cerned. I was quite a lot younger than he, which none of the other people he had outlived and triumphed over had been. As some profoundly narcissistic characters do, he merged with me to a considerable extent, rather than forming an ordinary neurotic transference. The fusion produced pseudo-projective identifica-tions, so he became convinced that *I* would suddenly die, and he never could tell whether he most feared, or wished for, this event. He envied me, he hated me, but, worse, he feared defeat in the life-or-death battle. Yet, really, that was the only prospect: the ending, or death, of either of us would have spelt defeat. The continuing analytic work, such as it was, was a dreadful sort of Pass-time, such as one might do in the ante-room to Hell. Al-though he was desperate to get away from me, he held on grimly and forced *me* to bring the subject up. In the end, I admitted defeat, whatever he feared, and said I was not prepared to go on. It was not by any means an exemplary Ending, as he spent most of the intervening weeks before he finally stopped screaming with rage, or sobbing, also with rage. His behaviour served only to strengthen my resolve. I am afraid he aroused only the most marginal sympathy in me. He demanded another analyst but could not begin to describe the person he now thought would be right for him. I refused anyway, because of my decision about his unanalysability and also out of compassion for whoever might land him next. What I did do was offer to refer him to a good behaviour therapist; the grinding, addictive monotony of his symptom struck me as being obsessional in quality, and there were also other features that were. He accepted this offer and then could hardly wait to be off. I did not hear from him again.

What did I learn from that experience?—I suppose, to withstand chronic hatred and contempt. Also, I realized how difficult it is to be heard as a valued interpreter when one is the object of true hatred and envy. I learned about certain narcissistic features, and how resistant to analysis they are. And I really became convinced that, in spite of what some people say, including analysts, analysis can*not* treat "anything", given time and the so-called "correct" interpretations. This idea is one of omnipotent lunacy. Freud certainly did not think so. He has a wonderful phrase somewhere about "low and repellent characters who are good for nothing in this world". I never discovered whether anything else underlay that patient's choice of death as his object of dread—or perhaps I should say, whether it was truly an existential dread, or was about something else as well, or primarily. I also learned that the prospect of inevitable death can make life itself a living death for some few unfortunates. Had I known about the theory and techniques of Self-psychology then, I might have treated him differently from the beginning. But it had not yet appeared on our scene.

Death should be a "concern" of all human beings. It crops up often, in various guises, in our work, and should therefore be reflected upon by analytic psychotherapists, apart from the fact that it is not going to spare us. The opposite extreme to the man I have described is met with more often—the variations of denial. There is actually a Society in America about which I read a long article a few months ago; it is composed of people who are going to live forever. I am perfectly serious—at least, about their belief. I am not referring to the cryonics group—the ones who get themselves frozen so that in the unlikely event of a cure being found for whatever they die of, plus a rejuvenating process, they can be unfrozen and resuscitated. This is a gruesome thought, as well as being, I believe, seriously mad. These are extreme variations of what people will do to avoid concern with the inevitable. The ones who propose to beat death altogether—the Live Forevers—believed that they had, if I remember aright, a mutated gene that had only recently appeared in mankind, which ensured this eternal journey. I am not at all sure how one knew if one had it, or what, besides living forever, it was said to promise; all the members of the Society—about sixty of them—were less than 45 years of age and presumably had not thought through the horror-filled possibilities of continuing to show ever-increasing signs of ageing without the often welcome rescue of death. Was it not extraordinary that they found each other, in a comparatively small area in the West of the United States? And will the Magic Gene protect them from runaway buses, or from those level crossings where a surprising number of individuals seem to arrive at the exact same moment as a train?

I believe that there is another way of approaching death— a strong and resilient Middle Way between denial and terror. Eschatology, or the study of last things, is not fashionable at present, at least not under this, its old name, and has not been for a century or more. Nevertheless, death is not quite the forbidden subject that it was even a few years ago. Bereavement counselling can almost be said to be one of the fashionable bandwagons, and this is on the whole a good sign, although unfortunately a rather mechanical quality inheres in the developing technique. In the heyday of Western Religion, from about the twelfth century to the mid-nineteenth, death—and particularly what was referred to as "a good death"—was one of the most important subjects of study and attention. Islam and Christianity offered a confident belief in eternal life, of peace and happiness, as a reward for a courageous, good life on earth. It was seen as a compensation for the widespread suffering that was accepted as part of most people's lot here below, in what Gray, in his Elegy, called "the short and simple annals of the poor". Eternal life was to be spent in the presence of God, and it was the encounters with God, Jesus, the Blessed Virgin, and the Communion of Saints that were faithfully anticipated, in a metaphysically vague place called Heaven. Those of you who know your Bible quite well may recall, however, that it, and particularly the New Testament, where one might expect it, has remarkably little to say about Heaven. Jesus himself concentrated more on living this life, and it is only in the Revelation of St. John the Divine that there is anything descriptive. This is so extraordinary, with its jewelled floors and strange mythical creatures, that one is left with the feeling that it would be extremely uncomfortable. Cultural themes have changed radically in this century, and people tend to be more self-conscious, atheistic, agnostic, and conditioned to thinking about notions such as *time*; an earthbound awareness of time can give the impression that an afterlife, were such a thing possible, would be one of intolerable and endless boredom.

However, this idea of dreadful boredom in the believer's heaven may in itself contribute to something positive about the non-believer's view of death. Although I am also reminded of Sam Goldwyn's classic answer to the question: "How's life?" "Not so bad", he said, "when you think of the alternative." What I mean by a "positive" contribution is that there is something appealing in the idea of simply stopping, as opposed to an unimaginable change of circumstances in which nevertheless consciousness, as we know it, always seems to persist. A strong and resilient Middle Way, of which I spoke, consists at least in part of a regular contemplation of the very *fact* of death, so that we familiarize ourselves with it. A discipline of simple meditation as part of one's life makes this sort of approach unalarming, partly because it increases calmness and detachment from the importance of the self.

Many people who are ignorant of Buddhism think that they know at least one thing about it and bring up the subject of reincarnation: as a matter of fact—as with most views and opinions on anything requiring blind faith, which is not a feature of Buddhist teaching—an open mind is maintained. Fanciful ideas of many lives with a clearly defined self, or coming back as an insect if one has not been good, are either fantasies projected into Buddhism by the uninstructed or derivations from some of the mythology that grows up around any religion. There is a central, and somewhat esoteric teaching, which is very much at the heart of Buddhist understanding of life, which is to do with egolessness; this, as *No-Self*, is said to be one of the Three Signs of Being, the other two being *Impermanence* and *Suffering*. Since it took me about twelve years before I really began to appreciate this teaching about egolessness or *No-Self*, I am certainly not going to embark on it here; but perhaps a glance may suggest that where ego does not exist and is fundamentally only the result of conditioning, the notion of dying would of necessity be different, to say the least. Briefly, the teaching on death tells us that life itself is an energy, which is inextinguishable; but the metamorphosis of personality and of the self is embroidery. Of course, understanding that the ego is a delusion adds a certain humour to practising Western psychological disciplines, in which we try to strengthen the ego. But I do also believe that one has to have a strong "conceptual ego" before one can confidently set about losing it!

The simple act of contemplating one's own death does much to contribute to peace of mind in the here and now; and when you come to think about it, the here and now is all there is for anyone—ever. There is nothing more liable to banish anxiety than to accept the inevitable with one's whole heart and to practise living only in the here and now.

We must re-focus our vision and move to a consideration of a particular concern of our own; though on a smaller scale, on reflection it may be considered to have in common many of the points I have made about the prospect of death and the fact of dying. I refer to the termination of a long and complex treatment by analytic psychotherapy. I am not aware of this particular comparative view having been made before, which—since it now seems to me rather obvious—I hope will not feel egregiously strained or exaggerated. I wonder if perhaps it has occurred to some (it has certainly cropped up in more than one analysis that is working towards an ending), but they may have held back from exploring it because of some anxiety about being accused of extremeness or even grandiosity. Also, I observe occasionally that even a mature, level-headed, and commonsensical person may have an almost superstitious fear of talking about death, and this would certainly include any comparative reference to death in connection with such a frequent phenomenon as ending a treatment in our own professional lives. Endings are a regular part of these lives, and they can present a wide range of problems. It is just as well to have an idea what some of these can be; there is little advantage during the termination stage in being taken by surprise, and a happening that might otherwise induce alarm and despair can be calmly surveyed if anticipated, or at least, made familiar in outline and expectation.

When the newly qualified therapist is freed from the fairly relentless input of supervisors, reading, clinical seminars, and lectures (all of which condition one to think about analytic therapy in certain ways without questioning) it may occur to one, at some point—perhaps not until one has negotiated the Ending of one's own personal analysis—that really, some of the things we do are very *odd*. I think this applies to ending the treatment. We have clothed the oddness in theory, technique, and familiarity; we discuss the interesting clinical phenomena of the termination phase in matter-of-fact voices; there are symposia on Criteria for Termination, and so on. All this material tends to disguise the oddity to which I refer, which is the fact of ending at all. Consider: analysts join with their prospective patients, after a careful and searching preliminary interview (itself probably following a long assessment by someone else) and between them they agree on a treatment contract; the treatment is usually prolonged, and is said, quite justifiably, to be one of the most important relationships of one's life. The patient will, under good-enough circumstances, become deeply, if ambivalently, attached to the therapist, both through the transference and through the real relationship, which by the time termination is decided upon will be quite extensive and will occupy some of the sublimated libidinal energy freed up by the preceding work. This complex attachment to the therapist is welcomed and, up to a point, reciprocated: indeed, although the therapist's personal involvement is more shadowy and delicate, it has to be authentic, in my view, or else the therapy does not truly "take" at the deepest levels. False selves and phoniness are part of psychopathology, and the patient does not need to encounter them in his therapist as he works away at the painful business of outgrowing his own and becoming responsible for genuine human intercourse. All levels of object-relating, closeness, intimacy, etc. are at the very heart of analytic therapy. The patient ceases to suffer in his ways of relating—at least often he does—and the acute, but passing, pains of insight take over from the personality problems presented at the beginning. Defences, of course, may have taken years to build up and are only slowly dismantled where unnecessary, to be supplanted by ego itself and by defences that are more resilient and healthy. Profound, moving, and significant conversations take place. The most casual observer would have no difficulty in noting that here is a relationship of great richness and importance. Such an observer might come to understand that this absorbing relationship is often experienced as the central feature of the patient's *life*. Emotions are withdrawn from other cathected object-relations as if to feed the analysis, and it is an utterly serious statement if patients say, as they sometimes do, something on the lines of: "For the moment, my analysis is my life." So what do we do? We bring it to an absolute end. And it is not an exaggeration to say that although they *know* that this will happen, some patients experience the agreement to end as a death sentence.

The untutored observer might react with shock. He would watch as a period of considerable disturbance ensues, but he would observe also, at one and the same time, that both therapist and patient take something about the situation for granted; of course, there may be massive protest, that is what the disturbance is all about, but curiously it seems to be contained within a framework of—not exactly acceptance, but something that is acutely paradoxical—resigned yet fighting, striving for freedom yet arguing against the agreement to stop, pleased yet anguished. The therapist, overall, can be observed to be constantly restoring and re-restoring a negotiated equilibrium, driving steadily towards a shared, whole-hearted point in time, consciously agreed upon by both parties, when this complex, deeply related couple split apart forever. It is the ultimate paradox. Yet what else can happen? What options are there? The natural, expectable progress of such a deep relationship, in what we call "real life", would be for it to go on and continue to enrich us. But although the patient spends part of the last few months elaborating fantasies around this prospect, he mostly knows they are fantasies. The therapist's time is not infinitely elastic. By now, over thirty years, I suppose someone like myself, who has always run a full-time mixed analytic and psychotherapy practice, has probably treated at some depth several hundred people. Life admits of the continuity of such a phenomenon only in limited sequences, certainly not in parallel.

The totality of the ending, which seems to go against the grain of all our work on love, loyalty, object-constancy, and intimacy, is reinforced by the austere prescription of no social contact thereafter. Thus we create an arbitrary situation that has much in common with a death. I am very much in favour of strict adherence to this rule, and I am quite willing to explore it with anyone who feels doubtful or confused as to its rationale. Features that recommend it include the reinforcement of the strength of internal objects; a refusal to expose, and perhaps impose, too much of the therapist's real self on vulnerable ex-patients; and granting them a freedom to work through and resolve final transferences, in fact, all remaining problems, on their own. It also allows patients to be sad and manage their own mourning for the loss.

I stand by this rule strongly myself, partly because, having experienced death in my early life and worked on it extensively during my analysis, I needed to handle this mourning alone, which is the only authentic way; this finally achieved a resolution that had never come about in my early adolescence and *could not now have come about* in the presence of the "lost object"—i.e. my analyst. But also I have seen a number of badly fumbled attempts by analysts or therapists who attempt to establish a post-therapy relationship with the patient, of whatever sort; the work of the therapy itself may be grossly undermined, and there can be no experience of completeness; there is an unsatisfactory lack of distinction in the ex-patient's mind between the absolute ending to the unique professional relationship and residual transferences that may never be fully recognized as such if the analyst subsequently presents wholly as a real person. This presentation puts a ban on the sort of patient-oriented exploratory talk that he/she has been accustomed to; and frequently disastrous regressive states set in. The commonest of these is a bitter vengefulness on the part of the patient; this is often suppressed, out of shame, yet I truly believe it could have been avoided; if one comes across this, one can be sure that either the therapy was not an overall success or, more likely, that there have been botched attempts at what the therapist may well have thought of as a more "human" relationship after the treatment. I believe that this idea is a fallacy and is always doomed to fail. It is unreal and injurious to the ex-patient insofar as the ending is wrenched away by the therapist from the necessary similarity to death.

The signs and symptoms of the termination period, which should ideally be, like gestation, about nine months, make a lot more sense immediately when we see that often the patient is protesting at the very point I have been making—that is, the existential and human irrationality of what we are doing is bringing the relationship to an end. Because certainly, even if the patient has been in full control of the date, the timing, the very fact of ending, there is a phase when it *feels* as though it is the therapist's doing. Projection can undermine intention. However, it is as well to pay the closest attention to the ending of one's own therapy. It sounds rather cold-blooded, but by then one *should* be in a position to study, as well as experience it. One should have learned enough detachment.

During termination, there is a particular sign or set of phenomena that may come about, and to a young therapist experiencing them for the first time they can be extremely unnerving. It is as if all the hard-won ground is lost. Suddenly, in place of the open, mature, balanced individual with whom we are able to discuss ending, there is a weeping, angry, bitter, scathing, jealous child, who may in addition be wheezing, or scratching, or shitting, or threatening suicide from black incomprehensible depression. I have lumped together here a number of symptoms that may have presented at the start of treatment, in different individuals, particularly those with psychosomatic symptoms, all long in abeyance by the end, mastered by insight and work and the facilitating environment. They sound monstrous when lumped together like this, but any previous long-forgotten symptom can be pretty horrifying when unexpectedly cropping up alone. Our hearts may faint within us, especially near the beginning of our professional lives, but it is now that a cool head and endurance are called for, alongside the mustering of our analytic skills to their utmost—and last but not least, hanging on to that faith in the *process* of analysis, and in ourselves, that I so often speak of.

This display of acute regression into a symptom-laden state, a repetition of the early days of their own history in analysis, is a complicated state, which, nevertheless, is similar in presentation from one patient to the next and tells us a number of similar things. It is as if there is a sort of secret sharing of knowledge, among patients, of a final common pathway. There is often fear, rather suddenly, of being abandoned into aloneness—in other words, fear of the bereavement that lies ahead. There may be a punishing wish to frighten the analyst, to show him up, to demonstrate that he has been fooled, as well as inept. This often occurs in patients who have never quite resolved an infantile ambivalence. It is a final kick in the direction of a bad internal object from childhood or youth, as if recognizing that this is a last permitted opportunity to take a bit of revenge. This particular interpretation is of considerable value at this point and may finally resolve the primitive ambivalence. There is also, rather strangely, a deep reluctance to bid farewell to these wild and childish parts of the self. At the same time, these demonstrations are a kind of leave-taking ceremony, in the presence of the only person who is likely to tolerate them, let alone understand them. For better or for worse, this, too, is the patient's self, though a self that is usually now carefully stored away in the archives.

It is an exhilarating time; the therapist must have all his wits about him and use them as never before, especially, I believe, in strengthening his resolve not to extend the duration of therapy. Often, in the midst of regression, there is a pitiful pleading, "Couldn't we extend, just till Christmas?" or "I know I'd be able to work it all out properly, if I had another six months." On the ultimate level, this is all baloney; if one gives in, six minutes would be about as valuable as six months; one has to sit it out and continue to work. Nor do I think anything advantageous occurs if one yields to the much rarer request to end sooner than planned. Unless a realistic and practical need is obvious, there is something going on that needs analysing, not collusion. I have recently wondered whether there is any comparison to be drawn with euthanasia and have not yet come to a conclusion. I would be concerned about a patient who suddenly got up and went off, thus trying to pre-empt the ending, illusorily snatching away control. Most patients by this time will in fact be sufficiently analysed to express the impulse verbally rather than act on it. However, the odd one who enacts it provides an opportunity for discovering how vital it is to have faith in the work *oneself* before, and during, the termination period. Patients are extremely perceptive about us, both consciously and unconsciously, and will spot and exploit a wavering of confidence and a readiness for anxiety. I believe that no effort should be spared to get a patient *back* who has done a runner at this point; forget your dignity and analytic persona and work at the primary task, before the patient's pride gets him stuck in an irredeemably damaging position.

The only concession I make to pleas for extra time, or brilliant ideas for friendship, or meeting socially, or even having an affair when therapy is over is to make it clear that if ever people are in real trouble or have a problem patch in their lives, the door will be ajar for them to come back and do a piece of work, provided I can offer some space—say, one or two sessions or half a dozen or so. Once a terminating patient, in a receptive, non-regressed mood, has taken this in thoroughly, it is surprising how rarely it needs to be used. And if the offer *is* taken up, then the time is always fruitfully used, taking advantage of all the mutual deep understanding and the shorthand developed during the treatment. Repair can usually be achieved very soon. Similarly, I have observed more than one example of a person with a terminal illness, who has been clearly told by an experienced physician that he has only a short but well-defined period of life left to him, who rather suddenly carries out some searching introspection, usually in conjunction with talking to a close friend. Very often, quite unexpectedly, someone who has never practised a religious discipline or developed any particular philosophy of life or death for himself may reach a thought-through position of calm acceptance and peace of mind, which will then sustain him—and those around him—to the end, without anxiety or denial. This is very impressive, as is also a patient who moves towards termination with appropriate affect and full use of all the preceding therapeutic work.

To go on for too long is a technical sin in our work, so I will reach my ending with the final abruptness that all patients, including ourselves, experience at the ending of their therapy, however well they have prepared the ground, and however inevitable it is.

CHAPTER TEN

The baby
and the bathwater

The difficulties with both bathwater and babies have some-thing in common; we forget our bathwater, and we do not exactly have to "remember" our babies; we may know them intimately, in almost every aspect of their being, but it would be hard to define them or describe their properties, or even really to explain what it is about them that makes them special to us. Nevertheless, the phrase swam into my mind, a while ago, as carrying an appropriate message for one looking back over a life, more than half of which has been spent being a psychoanalyst. Even before I began to think it out, I was aware that a lot of "stuff" had accumulated, starting long ago; and yet I certainly have not felt that I have been lumbering through life increasingly heavy-laden, as surely I would have if it had all stayed on board; some of it would even have disproportionately magnified the burden by fighting for space against deeply incompatible other things. With-out having really conceived of it in this way before, I realized I must have junked a lot of it as I went along, sometimes as a result of quite complicated, long-drawn-out, and occasionally difficult thinking. Those onomatopoeic words, flotsam and jetsam, have always appealed to me, though I could not imagine how I might ever use them. I used not to be able to remember how they differed, or how you told them apart. I am still not sure about telling them apart if you actually find them, but flotsam is goods resulting from a shipwreck and found floating in the sea, and jetsam is goods thrown overboard, or jettisoned. Just to complicate matters, *Chambers Dictionary* adds that jetsam also "according to some, is goods from a wreck that *remain under water*" (my italics, because I suddenly saw that the unconscious is the store for some of those). I do not, on looking, see many experiences in my life that were akin to shipwrecks, so this leads me to think that, although some may have remained under water, most of my abandonings—the result, I like to believe, of thought and choice—were jetsam. I have voluntarily jettisoned things, as one does the bathwater. No doubt many of the properties still inherent in the baby are flotsam, however.

It is not exactly normal to look upon an Oxford degree as so much bathwater; but, really, mine was. It was perfectly heavenly to be in at the time, and I loved every minute of it; the only drawback to it was that it was in Modern Languages, and in spite of my pleasure and relief at getting into Oxford on the only subjects my education had fitted me for, I was, in the long run, determined to be a doctor. Many was the time I heard it said to me afterwards: "But what a waste; don't you regret it?" I got so used to this that in the end I just said no. I grew weary of explaining, or trying to, that whatever one actually studied at Oxford was not what Oxford was about. Unless that was self-evident, I was not out to prove anything or convince people. It was much odder, in the event, that it was only when I did finally qualify as a doctor that I realized that I did not really want to be one—not a proper doctor, that is. Nothing that I have done since has, in fact, required it, except the two obligatory house jobs to get on the register and three years in a big psychiatric hospital, which was one of the most absorbing and vivid experiences of my life. It was not necessary to be a doctor to train as a psychoanalyst, *pace* Ernest Jones and some of the older doctor–analysts who could always produce an argument that suggested one made a "better analyst" if one were. It was only during my analysis that I understood the strong identification that had carried me so tenaciously through the medical training. What a lot of bathwater streamed away following my years and years of education!

It must be difficult for some analysts, and analytic therapists, to imagine exactly how utterly ignorant of psychoanalysis I was when I finally lurched into it. Many people who undertake an analysis and a training have been raised in a culture that means it is already deeply familiar to them at an early age. Some of them read Freud in their teens. I had hardly heard of him in my 30s. If one can be said to have to jettison ignorance, and as fast as possible, then that is what I did. And by the time I embarked on the training, I had also jettisoned Christianity, which had played an important role in my life until my late 20s. One can miss Christianity considerably on abandoning it, without any temptation to try to retrieve it. Loss of faith and a growing critical attitude to Christian doctrine mean that one cannot tread that path again. Out of the critical attitude there grew one feature that I really understood before I encountered psychoanalysis, and that was projection; once one begins to explore the extent to which the maintenance of Christianity in the culture depends upon the unconscious needs and projections of the faithful, there is no turning back. It is the hardest thing in the world to re-project something that one has truly withdrawn and acknowledged as one's own. The questions of morality, and on what it is based when God is dead, have occupied far greater minds than mine, but they are questions that require serious thought when one jettisons a religion that offers one a moral teaching, itself contingent upon the doctrines one is leaving behind. It may well be that the so-called "religious temperament", which I believe myself to have, is, *au fond*, a concealed wish to be inside a structure upon which one can depend for a moral system, rather than the continual lonely experience of self-reliance for one's every decision with a moral dimension. This was undoubtedly part of the appeal of Buddhism, which I came to some years later and have never felt the need to jettison—especially as it seems to blend so harmoniously on many levels with what by then I had taken on board of psychoanalysis.

And what of psychoanalysis itself? There is surely both flotsam and jetsam in one's long years of relationship with it. For example, I think, far from it being some subtle advantage to an analyst to be a doctor already, an early task facing doctors is one that lay-students do not encounter. One has to learn to forget that one *is* a doctor, and those years of quite strong conditioning do not easily turn into so much expendable bathwater. Maybe when doctoring was acquired later than usual, and with a struggle, there is even a proportionately greater cathexis of its style and meaning. They had their value in the social hierarchy. Doctors—even today, when in numbers alone they are outstripped by managers in the N.H.S. bureaucracy—have considerable power. They become accustomed, even as students, to knowing a great many rather esoteric things, to carrying authority, to being respected and obeyed. Some doctors, quite early on, become complacent and rather superior, as if it is something inherent in *them* that patients are in awe of, and not the role they have stepped into and the smattering of lore they have acquired. Doctors bring reassurance to the anxious; one only has to observe the almost palpable wave of relief when a doctor arrives at the scene of an accident, to appreciate that. They are needed quite openly when people are ill, or hurt and frightened. The task facing the new young doctor-analyst is, first, to accommodate the fact that none of this is necessarily true about a prospective patient's encounter with an analyst; and then to decide whether the conditions that people bring to her to "treat" are illnesses in the medical sense to which she has become accustomed—and if not, as I decided, how is her "treatment" going to differ from the kinds of thing she is used to handing out (down?) to her patients? It is clear that many analysts, starting with Freud, did—and do, though it is rarer now—see the conditions of human misery they meet as illnesses, and they carry didactic, authoritarian behaviour over into their analytic practice.

It is, I am sure, due to this that there used to be—and to a certain extent, still is—a "correct" way of doing the psychoanalytic version of psychotherapy, starting with the very first meeting. I have expressed elsewhere my strong criticism of analysts who carry out assessment consultations in almost unrelieved, unbending, "analytic" silence (Coltart, 1993). And from my training years, during the early 1960s, we certainly emerged, as fledgling analysts, sure that not only had we grasped the pure gold of true analytic knowledge, but that we knew how that knowledge should properly be imparted, in all circumstances; the patients should attend sessions five times a week, and lie on the couch; they should respect and accommodate our holidays, and they should pay us our required fee, including for missed sessions, whatever the reasons. And they should try at all times to tell us everything that comes into their minds. Not only is this now, mercifully, something of a caricature (but not necessarily so in all cases), but cursory inspection shows that it is, crudely speaking, in the style of the medical model. They must do what we tell them. I have forgotten to add that some patients were warned, but most were not, that they would not find us chattering to them, or answering questions, once treatment had started, but that our communications would be mainly limited to "interpretations", as from our Olympian height we gazed penetratingly into their unconscious worlds. I particularly want to criticize the rather loose, brief way of referring to "free association" as just described. Patients cannot possibly tell us everything in their minds, and it is a confused and unattainable ideal that we present in these words. On the contrary, a patient in analysis has to learn to scan the rich, ever-moving thoughts and feelings, and to *select* those that have more sense of pressure attached to them—*or*, of course, the ones that have apparently suddenly erupted from nowhere in the current context, and may seem to be peculiarly out-of-place and irrelevant. There is a real artistic skill to be learned here.

In learning to jettison much of the medical model to which I had only recently become accustomed, I was forced to begin to think out what the differences now were; this was salutary and interesting and continued on and off for years. I realized, and continued to use, the idea that rather than being in a powerful position of authority to one who was, in many ways, down some scale from me, my relationship to my patients (a word I still like, since it means "suffering" and has only been ignorantly politicized into becoming undesirable) was one of "equality but asymmetry". It is no good pretending, with false humility, as do some over-politicized therapists, that we have no special knowledge or technique, nothing that the patient wants or needs. Clearly we have, else we would not be offering something and charging fees for it. Quite early on, I jettisoned any lingering notion that psychoanalysis was a true science, and I joined the ranks of those who see it as an art and a craft—one of the humanities. Of course, it also has certain similarities, both in structure and in its practitioners, to religion, and this has not been helped, or modified, by some leading figures over the years who seem to have been what Lomas (1994) has called "fishers of men", interested in obtaining converts and devotees to their faith or to themselves. Ivan Ward, the Director of the Freud Museum, edited a short book (1992), entitled, *Is Psychoanalysis Another Religion?* to which I contributed a chapter trying to demonstrate, among other things, how some people—both patients and analysts—very much want it to be and treat it as if it were. Probably my years as a Christian, and my need to think through my jettisoning of that, protected me from this danger.

Part of the medical model that had to be abandoned was a sort of conviction in the analytic air that "real" psychoanalysis could somehow only happen if the patient attended for four or five sessions a week. A few years in practice, with a number of patients attending once or twice a week, soon serve to clear one's mind of this erroneous conviction and make one realize that its emphasis is in the wrong place in any case. What matters, alongside the increasing flexibility of one's own technique, is the quality of psychological-mindedness in the patient. It is perfectly possible for someone who, for many and various reasons, can only come once a week to "have" psychoanalysis. The depth of the unconscious that can be reached, the subtle shorthands that develop between the two, and the working-through capacities of a committed and psychologically minded patient leave one in no doubt about this. (There is, in any case, a not shallow way of defining psychoanalysis as "What psychoanalysts do in their consulting-rooms", though I can see dangers inherent in this definition.) Furthermore, the intensity, vividness, and expressive communications of some people's body and facial language soon confirm one's decision that it was right to jettison the idea that all patients must lie on the couch. Freud openly said that it was instituted because he did not like being stared at all day, so any insistence that it is entirely for the patients' benefit soon wears thin. I believe, too, that one has to clear one's mind as early as possible on the subject of what an analytic therapy is *for*. While fully subscribing to—and I think by now understanding—Bion's prescription that one should work without memory or desire, I also believe that one needs to develop a philosophy of treatment and protect oneself and one's patients from the vague, meandering analyses that go on for years and years—anything up to twenty or more. If one believes that people truly want to be living happier, less anxiety-ridden, and more fulfilling lives, then one will be pointed in the direction that the more they have of them (away from treatment), the longer they can be happy for, and the less they need to go through being dependent on us, the better. Most analysts can cite some examples—I do not mean from their own practices, but on the circuits of "professional patients"—of people who have had, and are still having, two or three lengthy analyses, so that in the end they will have spent anything up to fifty years on couches. What *can* they be hoping for? And ought we not to avoid colluding with them—especially with those who also practise as analysts or therapists? Have they any hope of becoming truly independent selves before they die?

In this context, I have found it valuable not to remain too benightedly in ignorance of other theories and therapies that have evolved alongside our own; the (unconscious?) proclamation that we know that our theory and practice is Best so easily merges with a narcissistic conviction that we who practise it are Best. Our ever-growing literature is not Holy Writ, but an often interesting, instructive, and creative body of work that has grown out of the psychoanalytic century. But there is a lot to learn from literature beyond our own; I am thinking here of psychosynthesis and the work of Assagioli in particular. What appealed to me about him is his inclusion and treatment of the will—which he termed "the Cinderella of modern psychology". Although Freud *implied* that patients should use their wills in order to play their part in psychoanalysis responsibly, he rarely said so directly. Assagioli's book *The Act of Will* (1994) repays reading. The psychoanalytic movement encouraged, in a way that Freud did not necessarily intend, spontaneity and free expression of emotions that nineteenth-century morality had required to be repressed. By now the results of this have turned into a ludicrous—if it were not sad and alarming—travesty of itself: a longing to find, know, and express more of the true self has become a widespread sense of having "rights" to all sorts of things, for example, instant gratification of one's more infantile demands. Those who helped to unleash the "let-it-all-hang-out" approach of the 1960s now bewail the lack of boundaries and discipline in self-regulation that they see all around them. Psychoanalysis has little with which to counter this. Assagioli, an analyst from the early years of the century, developed a somewhat counter-analytic idea—namely, that the use of the self's resources was neglected if the properties of the will were ignored by the analysts. He describes them: energy, concentration, intensity, one-pointedness, initiative, courage, and mastery; he shows how their value as skills for fulfilled living can be developed; and he describes the "stages of willing", up to the realization of planned, not idealized, goals. One does not really have to throw out anything, beyond fanatical and narrow-minded loyalty to Freud, to see much of value in his writing. And of course it blends with attractive norms of self-reliance and moral responsibility.

I have often been surprised by people who seem to remember in considerable detail what their analyses were *about*. However, many do not, which is consoling. I belong to the latter group, though I remember deep currents of it, and the fact that it was a help to someone who took many emotional sequelae of a traumatized childhood into her treatment. My analyst had a real gift for working with bereavement and with long-term grief and rage and loss. However there were a number of facets to her language, theory, and thinking that I could not accept, and never have; I remember thinking that I would simply need to evolve and do things differently when my turn came. In fact, it came early, as I set up my private practice in the second year of my analysis, after four years in the N.H.S. My analyst had had an extremely classical training—and not enough of it, as I occasionally told her!—in that she went to Freud for two years just after World War I, and subsequently to Melanie Klein for a year in England. Distinguished as these forbears may be, I neither wished to be like them, nor does one receive grace handed down, as it said to be through the Apostolic Succession in the Church. I was her last student, and she was over 70 when I qualified; much of her language and theory were alien to me, though I have to assume that my unconscious could translate what it needed. Probably the fact that I was so green when I started had a paradoxical effect—in one way I was a *tabula rasa* ready to receive news, and yet, in another, my "resistances" may have preserved me from an over-identification with her style and orientation. I could evolve my own, while being fundamentally legitimized to practice psychotherapy rooted in the dynamic tradition. Theory does affect technique, but so, extensively, does the personality of the therapist, and I did not feel I became—nor did she want me to—a clone of my analyst, as I have observed happening to some students.

There was plenty of creative writing appearing at the time to feed the baby, who was the growing analytic therapist in me. Anyway, it struck me that the patient, in the eyes of Freud and Klein, was seen as a passive sort of object, rather at the mercy of impersonal, instinctual forces, thought to be universal; and also at the mercy of their interpretations as such, without much in the way of personal responsibility and moral choice.[1] A lot was talked about guilt, especially unconscious guilt; but I thought long ago, and I still believe today, that it is not necessary for guilt to be an ongoing emotion for the rest of one's life. If the developmental structure and behaviour of one's own superego was thoroughly understood, and the subject is living a life that voluntarily undertakes responsibility on all levels for herself, guilt is not an inevitable accompaniment. Often when people speak of feeling guilty, they mean shame, anyway, and this, too, needs attentive analysis. Several analysts have argued this point with me, but I still believe that peace of mind and a guilt-free existence are legitimate aims of a psychodynamic therapy. Nevertheless, there is a way of constantly provoking self-responsibility in a patient, which can be overdone during a therapy, and I have at times been horrified, when taking seminars, to listen to unremitting onslaughts by some students on their patients. There is a school of analytic thought that seems to have the effect on an inexperienced student of making her "show" the regressed patient, continually, his greed, hostility, and envy, which through the "transference" is said to be directed at the omnipotent, all-giving breast, the analyst. The students themselves display the anxious subservience that this technique induces, and, presumably as compensation, become grandiose and bullying with their patients. This type of analysis manifests another feature about which I have written before (Coltart, 1993) and which relates to technique. The students reveal during their clinical presentations that they have not taken a history from the patient in the preliminary session and therefore work in ignorance of it, relying, as more than one has told me loftily or reprovingly, on "interpreting

---

[1] When I read my paper, "Slouching towards Bethlehem", to the very classical Society in Boston, one aged member said that he "didn't see much about *drives* in it". I had to reply: "No—there is nothing about drives in it."

the transference" and nothing else. Transference in the early months—and sometimes thereafter—may be extremely hard to read, and some of it is in any case an artefact of the unsatisfactory therapeutic situation just described; the "interpretations" thus are a blend of ill-absorbed theory and fantasy (the analysts' own, about the patient's infantile fantasy). I cannot repeat often enough how important I think it is to start a treatment armed with a good, detailed history. Even if this particular school of thought does not approve of reconstruction or genetic interpretations, transference itself is a product of history—at least, if people are to be respected as individuals at all. I acknowledge that my dislike of a lot that I saw may have caused me to jettison some few things that might have been valuable.

We are on a tightrope here (Coltart, 1992a) as we so often are. The dangers on the other side are met with more frequently in the world of counselling, or therapies with inadequate trainings, especially in relation to people who have allegedly been abused in childhood. The danger is that the patient is seen only as a victim. No doubt many were, but it is not a fruitful role to live out as a life, and a therapist who sides with the patient against the parental figures rather than gradually trying to understand them is, beyond a certain very limited point, of no therapeutic value to a patient. Any tendency in oneself to over-identify with the sufferings of a patient, especially against alleged inflictors of harm, has to be rooted out and left behind in the development of a strong technique. It does nothing to help the patient take responsibility for what she *has become and is now*, which may well be all that is left to an adult (quite apart from the considerable dangers of assisting in the production and cementing of false memories). What the patient is now, here in our room in her session, is how things are, and, though much may need working through, our job is to help her to live on from here. In fact, one needs to learn, early on, that anything much in the way of *expressed* sympathy and concern for the horrors of a patient's life is not technically valuable. A good doctor can make rich use of it as part of the healing process, and it is another thing that has to be re-thought and jettisoned. It sounds austere, but then in some ways, psychoanalysis *is* austere. As is Buddhism.

It would be impossible to list in detail all the many things that I have allowed to drain away, or voluntarily thrown overboard down the years. I want to make one more, perhaps controversial, point in connection with concepts or ideas that we continually need to scrutinize in order to see how many assumptions or *idées reçues* have crept into our repertoire. There may be things that need throwing away—or alternatively, on second thoughts, there may be something we want to retrieve. Such a one was the "corrective emotional experience". Rather vaguely, we all assimilated some notion that analysts do not offer this—whatever it means, it had an undesirable aura round it. If anything, we believed it meant "gratifying the patient", which we must not do. We probably have not read the classical paper by that name by Alexander and French (1946). We may only have had some sketchy ideas about Ferenczi, too, before reading his vivid and extraordinary *Clinical Diaries* (1989). Many therapists and analysts emerge from their training with a received idea that whatever it is, we do not give our patients Corrective Emotional Experience. I want to say now that I think this is rubbish. It needs understanding and re-thinking. Certainly I am not advocating some bizarre sort of sensual, or sexual, gratifying acting-in. Nor can we somehow become a real mother to their own infant-self. But, however much our patients differ, we can be sure that they are anxious and unhappy, and that they want improvements in these states and, if possible, release and healing. Without going beyond the boundaries of our treatment setting as we normally inhabit it, and without sentimental or emotional behaviour, we *are* offering our patients a corrective emotional experience in their therapy. Every therapy is, or should be, in my view, such an experience. I do not believe that this represents an unattainable ideal. Therapy is certainly an experience—one of the most important of one's life. It is certainly emotional—that is self-evident—and it is much more so for the patient, but the empathic therapist moves in the patient's shadow. And if it is not corrective, sessionally as well as in the long term, if there is not an atmosphere about it that is beneficial—even enjoyable—even to the patient who is suffering in the midst of something painful, then what are we up to? Why are we doing it? I think we have to jettison as soon as we can the idea that the sacred earnestness of our calling means that the patient—and the analyst—must not *enjoy* the session, and get something positive and healing just from being there.

There is a way of thinking about every therapy as a long, slow jettisoning of a lifetime's bathwater, allowing the emerging baby to come to know herself, her inner selves, her false selves, and grow into a truer and happier self. It is important that we are aware of what and who our own self-baby became, and how and why. We may even be surprised, when we begin to think about it, just how much bathwater, which for a while we may have lain in happily and which we needed, we have managed to jettison during the course of our lives.

You may have noticed that I have said relatively little about the baby in this essay, compared with the amount of varied things that have gone into the past as bathwater. This is deliberate. "The baby" is what I became, who I am, and is the source of all I have written in my three books, in and about my working life. Inevitably, when one writes in the way I do, which, when it is not a case history, is mainly free-associative thoughts on the experiences, and style, of a working therapist, one cannot help but give a quite detailed picture of oneself. In fact, it is important not to be afraid of doing so. The work of therapy is so intensely personal and, I believe, so influenced both in process and in outcome by who one is that to try to shrink into a corner or pretend that one is not intimately involved in every step on the way is a sort of false humility and does nothing to enhance the readability of what one is trying to express. In fact, I have always found that impersonal essays, especially on theory, are heavy and dull in proportion to their depersonalization, and I have never got much of value from them. It is, however, almost impossibly hard to imagine what readers will get from one's own essays, and I can only hope, as I come to the close of my writing life, that I have conveyed at least some of my own continual enjoyment in my work to those of you who have stayed with me to the end.

REFERENCES

Alexander, F. (1950). *Psychosomatic Medicine.* New York: W. W. Norton.

Alexander, F., & French, T. M. (1946). Gratifying the Patient. In: *Psychoanalytic Therapy.* New York: Ronald Press.

Assagioli, R. (1994). *The Act of Will.* Reprint. London: Aquarian/ Thorsons.

Bion, W. (1961). *Experiences in Groups and Other Papers.* London: Tavistock Publications.

Bollas, C. (1987). *The Shadow of the Object: Psychoanalysis of the Unthought Known.* London: Free Association Books.

Coltart, N. (1987). Diagnosis and Assessment of Suitability for Psychoanalytical Psychotherapy. *British Journal of Psychotherapy, 4* (2): 127–134.

Coltart, N. (1988). The Assessment of Psychological-Mindedness in the Diagnostic Interview. *British Journal of Psychiatry, 153*: 819–820.

Coltart, N. (1992a). On the Tightrope. In: *Slouching towards Bethlehem: And Further Psychoanalytic Explorations* (pp. 95–110). London: Free Association Books.

Coltart, N. (1992b). *Slouching towards Bethlehem: And Further Psychoanalytic Explorations.* London: Free Association Books.

Coltart, N. (1993). *How to Survive as a Psychotherapist.* London: Sheldon Press.

Crisp, A. H. (1963). Some Current Aspects of Psychosomatic Research. *Postgraduate Medical Journal, 39.*

Crisp, A. H. (1966). Evolution and Presentation of Anorexia Nervosa. *Proceedings of the Royal Society of Medicine, 58.*

Crisp, A. H. (1968). Some Approaches to Psychosomatic Clinical Research. *British Journal of Medical Psychology, 41.*

Engel, G. L. (1954). Studies of Ulcerative Colitis: The Nature of the Psychological Processes. *American Journal of Medicine, 16*: 496–501.

Engel, G. L. (1962a). Anxiety and Depression Withdrawal: The Primary Affects of Unpleasure. *International Journal of Psycho-Analysis, 43*: 89–97.

Engel, G. L. (1962b). *Psychological Development in Health and Disease.* Philadelphia, PA: Saunders.

Engel, G. L. (1967). Psychological Factors and Ulcerative Colitis. *British Medical Journal, 56*: 344–365.

Engel, G. L., & Schmale, A. H. (1967). Psychoanalytic Theory of Somatic Disorder. *Journal of the American Psychological Association, 15*: 344–365.

Ferenczi, S. (1988). *Clinical Diaries of Sandor Ferenczi* (ed. by J. Dupont; trans. by M. Balint & N. Z. Jackson). Cambridge, MA: Harvard University Press.

Freud, S. (1905d). *Three Essays on the Theory of Sexuality. S.E., 7.*

Freud, S. (1910c). *Leonardo da Vinci and a Memory of his Childhood, S.E., 11.*

Freud, S. (1910k). "Wild" Psycho-Analysis, *S.E., 9.*

Freud, S. (1912b). The Dynamics of Transference. *S.E., 12.*

Freud, S. (1913c). On Beginning the Treatment. *S.E., 12.*

Freud, S. (1914c). On Narcissism: An Introduction. *S.E., 14.*

Freud, S. (1914g). Remembering, Repeating and Working-Through. *S.E., 12.*

Freud, S. (1915a [1914]). Observations on Transference-Love. *S.E., 12.*

Freud, S. (1916–17). *Introductory Lectures on Psycho-Analysis. S.E., 15–16.*

Freud, S. (1924c). The Economic Problem of Masochism. *S.E., 19.*

Freud, S. (1927c). *The Future of an Illusion. S.E., 21.*

Freud, S. (1950a [1887–1902]). Project for a Scientific Psychology. *S.E., 2.*

Gillespie, W. (1956). The General Theory of Sexual Perversion. *International Journal of Psycho-Analysis, 37*: 396–403

Glover, E. (1933). The Relation of Perversion Formation to the Development of Reality Sense. *International Journal of Psycho-Analysis, 14*: 486–504.

Goldberg, J. (1989). A Shared View of the World. *International Journal of Psycho-Analysis, 70,* 16–20.

Guntrip, H. (1968). *Schizoid Phenomena Object Relations and the Self.* London: Hogarth. [Reprinted London: Karnac Books, 1996.]

Heimann, P. (1950). On Counter-Transference. *International Journal of Psycho-Analysis, 31*: 81–84.

Isaacs, S. (1930). *Intellectual Growth in Young Children.* London: Routledge & Kegan Paul.

Jackson, M. (1978). The Mind–Body Frontier: The Problem of the "Mysterious Leap". *Bulletin of the British Psychoanalytical Society, 6.*

Khan, M. M. R. (1963). Ego Ideal, Excitement and the Threat of Annihilation. *Journal of Hillside Hospital, 12*: 195–217.

Khan, M. M. R. (1974). *The Privacy of the Self.* London: Routledge. [Reprinted London: Karnac Books, 1996.]

King, P., & Steiner, R. (1992). *The Freud–Klein Controversies, 1941–1945.* London: Tavistock.

Lacan, J. (1977). *Ecrits: A Selection* (trans. A. Sheridan). London: Tavistock Publications.

Lee, R. R., & Martin, J. C. (1989). *Psychotherapy after Kohut.* Hillsdale, NJ: Analytic Press.

Lomas, P. (1993). *Cultivating Intuition. An Introduction to Psychotherapy.* Northvale, NJ: Jason Aronson. Harmondsworth, Middlesex: Penguin, 1994.

McDougall, J. (1974). The Psychosoma and the Psychoanalytic Process. *International Review of Psychoanalysis, 1.* [Reprinted in *Plea for a Measure of Abnormality* (pp. 337–396). New York: International Universities Press, 1980.]

McDougall, J. (1980). *Plea for a Measure of Abnormality.* New York: International Universities Press.

McDougall, J. (1989). *Theatres of the Body.* London. Free Association Books.

Meissner, W. (1992). *A Psychological Study of St. Ignatius of Loyola.* New Haven, CT: Yale University Press.

Milner, M. (1959). *The Hands of the Living God.* London: Hogarth.

Nemiah, J. C., Sifneos, P. E., & Freyberger, H. (1976). Alexithymia: A View of the Psychosomatic Process. In: O. Hill (Ed.), *Modern Trends in Psychosomatic Medicine, Vol. 3.* London: Butterworth.

Panel on Perversions (1954). *Journal of American Psychological Association.*

Pasche, F. (1964). Symposium on Homosexuality. *International Journal of Psycho-Analysis,*

Paulley, J. (1964). Asthma, Migraine and Ulcerative Colitis: For Each Disorder a Specific Psychotherapeutic Approach. Paper presented at International Congress of Psychotherapy, London.

Rycroft, C. (1968). *Imagination and Reality: Psycho-Analytical Essays, 1951–1961.* London: Hogarth Press. [Reprinted London: Karnac Books, 1987.]

Sants (1964). Genealogical Bewilderment. *British Journal of Medical Practice,*

Schmale, A. H., Jr. (1958). Relationship of Separation and Depression to Disease. *Journal of Psychosomatic Medicine, 20,* 259–277.

Schmale, A. H., Jr. (1964). Genetic View of Affects: With Specific Reference to the Genesis of Helplessness and Hopelessness. *Psychoanalytic Study of the Child, 19,*

Sperling, M. (1957). Psychoanalytic Treatment of Ulcerative Colitis. *International Journal of Psycho-Analysis, 38*: 341–349.

Stein, S. (1991). The Influence of Theory on the Psychoanalyst's Counter-Transference. *International Journal of Psycho-Analysis, 72,* 325–335.

Symington, N. (1993). *Narcissism: A New Theory.* London: Karnac Books.

Thera, Nyanaponika (1962). *The Heart of Buddhist Meditation.* London: Century Hutchinson.

Ward, I. (Ed.) (1992). *Is Psychoanalysis Another Religion?* London: Freud Museum Publications.

Winnicott, D. W. (1954). Metapsychological and Clinical Aspects of Regression within the Psycho-Analytical Set-Up. In: *Through Paediatrics to Psycho-Analysis.* London: Hogarth & The Institute of Psychoanalysis, 1975. [Reprinted London: Karnac Books, 1992.]

Winnicott, D. W. (1971). *Playing and Reality.* London: Tavistock Publications.

Wittkower, E. D. (1938). Ulcerative Colitis: Personality Studies. *British Medical Journal, II*: 1356.

Wittkower, E. D. (1967). The Psychogenic Component in Ulcerative Colitis. *Canadian Medical Association Journal, 97.*

INDEX

listening, 28–30, 123
living forever, 146
love, capacity for, 21, 38
    towards patient, 86
    in transference, 67

Martin, Denis, 1
masturbation, 7
McDougall, Joyce, 96, 169
meditation, 132, 134–135
memory and desire, 123
Middle Way, the, 130, 146
mind, 74–82
    as object, 75
    idealisation of, 78–79
    ruining life, 81
money, 26, 99, 105
moral sense, 118, 123, 131, 139
mother, 2, 5, 114
    having two, 1–22
    in transference, 10

narcissism, 70, 86, 89
    as personality disorder, 121–122,
        144
negative capability, 67
No–Self, 126–128, 133–134, 139,
    148

oak-tree, 78
Oedipus complex, 18, 19, 112
Oxford education, 156

patient, being a, 49, 55
    learning from the, 145
    "professional", 160
    unsuitable for psychoanalysis,
        143–144
perversion, 1–22, 170
    appearance in sessions, 12, 13,
        16
    partner in, 6
    preventing psychosis, 9
    theory of, 9
    uses of, 16
    professional identity, 45
pseudonym, 44
psychoanalysis:
    and Buddhism, 125–139
    contraindications, 98
    patients unsuitable for, 117, 143–
        144
    powerful instrument, a, 93
    "real", 33, 158
    student unsuitable for, 111
    termination of, 148–154

psychoanalyst(s), 24, 36
    being a, in a group, 44–57
    criticisms of, 33
    effects of saying one is a, 43, 48
    and human relations, 32
    magical powers of, 44
psychological-mindedness, 111, 120
psychosomatic illness, 92–108

quis custodiet?, 110

reparation, 35

scapegoat, 51
Scharff, David, 31
Scientology, 8
self, 115, 136, 138
    acting the, 81
    true and false, 81, 134
    as weapon, 82
shame, 85, 88, 138
smell, patients who, 86
sphinx, 51–52
Stein, Sam, 45
stories, 27
students, 163
suffering, 126–130
suggestion, 71
suicide, 87–89
supervision, 109–124
Symington, Neville, 32, 131, 170

termination of therapy, 148–154
transference, 57–73, 117
    cure, 64
    difficulties, 68, 71
    history, importance of, 62
    interpretation, 72
    neurosis, 66
    not pushing the, 58, 60
    as resistance, 60, 68

ulcerative colitis, 91–108
    symptoms, 100, 104, 106

unconscious, the, 34
    disbelief in, 35

vocation, 34, 36, 111

Ward, Ivan, 160
weapon, 79, 106
    self as, 82
Winnicott, D. W., 113, 134, 170
worries, 142
wounded healer, 35